GOODBYE

GoodBye

Yvonne Vissing

For those who did not have a choice

Copyright © 2025 by Yvonne Vissing. Published by the Initiative for Civility in Everyday Life.
All rights reserved. No part of this book may be reproduced in any manner whatsoever without written permission except in the case of brief quotations embodied in critical articles and reviews.
First Printing, 2025

Contents

Dedication		iv
1	The Goodbye Vision	1
2	Going My Way	10
3	Death is Relational and Transactional	19
4	The Disclosure Dilemma	32
5	The Life Review	42
6	Emotions and the Transactional Nature of Death	59
7	The Importance of Ceremonies	94
8	Death as a Business Transaction	116
9	Making A GoodBye For You and Others	152
10	Words of Wisdom	162
11	It's About You Workbook	166
12	Who Have You Been?	167
13	Your Family Tree	170
14	Your Jobs and Military Experience	173
15	Your Hobbies, Sports, and Recreation	176
16	Your Relationships	178
17	Pets and Animals	181
18	Where Have You Lived?	183
19	Your Travels	185

20	Who Are You Now?	187
21	Your Religious or Spiritual Life	190
22	When You Die	192
23	Burial Questions	195
24	Your Memorial Preferences	198
25	Who You Want To Come To Your Memorial Service	202
26	People You Don't Want	205
27	Love Letters	207
28	Peace Of Mind Letters	209
29	Letting Go Of Regrets	210
30	Your Good Deeds	217
31	Your Money and Wealth	220
32	Your Debts	224
33	Your Insurance	227
34	Your Stuff	231
35	Your Will	233
36	Your Obituary	236
37	Your Legacy	238

About the Author   239

1

The Goodbye Vision

The GOODBYE Vision

Life has a beginning, middle, and end.
Always.
For every living thing.
There will be an end to all of us.
But what's next?
We really don't know.
It will likely be amazing.

But it's scary, especially for us who like predictability.
For us who are control freaks.
Who want to exactly what is going to happen next.
We may not know many things, but we DO know that
there is the ONE certain thing
that we all know is going to happen.
We are going to die.

When and how are usually unknown ahead of time.
Death can come swiftly and unexpectedly.
Death can also be a long and challenging process, especially if we are ill.

We never know for sure when today will be our last day.

The when, why, and how details about our departure are something that we might want to spend a little time thinking about. Anticipation of our inevitable journey will help us to make a better going away experience for ourselves - and for those we leave behind. Prevention can reduce a lot of problems later on.

Death shouldn't be a surprise for any of us.
Life and death are hand-holding partners.
You can't have one without the other.

When people ask my friend Bernard "How are you?", he simply replies, "Slowly dying." This response always surprises people. He is young, healthy, and handsome, with his whole life unfolding ahead. Yet he always remembers that today and tomorrow are connected. For Bernard, to die well means that he has to live life to its fullest every day in every way.

Many people refuse to talk about dying.
It isn't something we like to think about.
It's uncomfortable.
We would rather focus on what we are doing later today.

Like Bernard, we might benefit from reflecting on how death informs life. But not everyone takes that route. My parents, for instance, didn't talk about their dying plans. They surely thought about it. They did create wills. They might mention things they liked, or didn't, about other people's funerals. But they didn't share information with us about what they needed or wanted for their own GoodBye. We had to guess. Like most people who are left behind, we made decisions that we wanted, or what we thought they might want, rather than decisions that they may have preferred.

The fact is that if we don't know what the dying (or dead) person wants, as the person who is put in the decision-making role, we are going to do what we think is best for them – and for ourself.

Most parents avoid end-of-life talks with their children, fearing they'll cause distress or spark conflict. Children may avoid this type of conversation with their parents for the same reasons. The Result: Nobody is talking about the elephant in the room.

Let's talk about why we avoid conversations about death.

We may love our families deeply—but that doesn't mean our relationships are easy. Many of us carry unspoken tensions or unresolved conflicts with family members, and as the end of life nears, the last thing we want is to ignite old fires. But our reluctance to talk about death often reflects more than just discomfort—it's rooted in a lifetime of emotional complexities that have gone unaddressed.

Conflict often bubbles to the surface when someone is dying. Parent-child tensions, sibling rivalries, and the hidden frictions between spouses—these are all normal and common. In blended families, where "yours, mine, and ours" live under the same roof (or across several), end-of-life decisions can become particularly messy. Differences in age, values, culture, and religion may further divide family members when unity is needed most.

Even with good intentions, communication often falters. People speak clumsily, hear imperfectly, and interpret emotionally. Misunderstandings are common. Criticism, defensiveness, and old wounds may cloud even the kindest efforts. Then there's the matter of money—a topic that can stir resentment, revive old grievances, or create new ones. Past financial decisions or perceptions of fairness can complicate current relationships. Disputes over how expenses are handled—or what's "owed"—can trigger explosive stress.

Families often carry a shared emotional history, complete with hurt, neglect, abuse, or trauma. These dynamics might have been buried for years, but major life transitions like death tend to bring them to the surface. Events and emotions we've worked hard to avoid may suddenly demand to be acknowledged.

But we don't have to carry that baggage all the way to the end.

We can choose to be the adult in the room—the one who models a healthier way forward. By addressing what we can now, we help smooth the path for those we love. A thoughtful, honest exit plan can become an act of healing. We can preserve the love that existed, nurture what still can be, and protect our family from unnecessary pain. A difficult past doesn't have to dictate the future—unless we bring it there.

The present offers us a powerful gift: the opportunity to break cycles of silence and conflict. Let's use it. As the saying goes, there is no day but today.

Death Across the Generations

Historically, children witnessed the full arc of life—from birth to death—within the family. Babies were born at home. Elders died surrounded by loved ones. Life and death weren't separate—they were chapters in the same story.

Today, those experiences are often hidden behind closed doors in hospitals or nursing homes. As a result, many children grow up shielded from death, and adults avoid the topic until they're forced to face it.

But pretending death isn't coming doesn't stop it from arriving.

While most parents assume they'll outlive their children, life doesn't always follow our hopes. My grandmother lived to be 101, and by then, she had buried three of her four children. Anthony's son died unexpectedly, and the family was thrown into turmoil—not just by grief, but by the confusion of trying to make final arrangements without knowing what he would have wanted. That kind of uncertainty only compounds heartbreak.

Many parents don't ask their children what they might want if the unthinkable were to happen. But opening that door—even gently—can lead to surprising and meaningful insights.

Merriweather, for example, talked with her teenage and young adult children about end-of-life wishes. What she learned astonished her. One child wanted to be buried in the family cemetery near the grandparents. Another wanted a green burial, imagining plants growing from their body. A third wanted their ashes scattered across four places around the world that held special meaning. None of these wishes would have been obvious—and none would have been honored had the conversation never happened.

We do our loved ones a real kindness by sharing what we want for our goodbye. And we honor them by asking what they might want as well. It's not an easy conversation. It's not like

planning a dream trip to Paris or Borneo. But if approached with calm, care, and transparency, it can become a profound expression of love and understanding.

Why wait?
As Fleetwood Mac sang:
Don't stop thinking about tomorrow. It will soon be here.

Too many people wait until the last minute to figure out their final wishes—if they ever get around to it at all. Most of us are too busy living to spend time thinking about dying. But if we don't speak up, those left behind will be forced to guess. And their guesses may lead to choices we wouldn't want.

Vanessa's daughter was only six years old when she was diagnosed with a terminal illness. As young as she was, she was still able to share her thoughts about what she wanted for her goodbye. Those conversations—though heartbreaking—brought clarity, comfort, and connection. After her passing, the family didn't fall apart; instead, they grew forward. Her memory lives on in their hearts, not as a wound, but as a light.

Most of us don't want people to feel broken when we leave this world. We want them to feel our love. We want them to smile at our memory, to feel grateful for the time we had together. We want to be remembered—not just for how we died, but for how we lived and touched each other's lives.

Let's make that possible. Let's talk now.

The Changing Nature of Funerals: Making A Good Goodbye
There's a quiet revolution happening around how we think about death. For generations, dying was treated as something sad, secretive, and best left unspoken. But that mindset has begun to shift.

Enter the **Death Positive Movement,** a growing social and cultural movement that asserts that our silence around death does more harm than good. Its advocates argue that by hiding death behind hospital doors and closed caskets, we isolate the dying, create unnecessary fear, and burden the living with confusion and unresolved feelings. Instead, they promote a transparent, inclusive, and even life-affirming approach to dying.

Talking about death doesn't have to be morbid—it can be deeply human. Death is the one thing that connects all living things. Acknowledging that reality doesn't diminish life; it deepens it.

The Death Positive Movement encourages individuals, families, and lawmakers to honor people's end-of-life wishes—environmentally, emotionally, spiritually, and practically. This means that you have a right to decide what happens to your body, how you are remembered, and who is involved in your farewell.

In fact, the movement has developed a Death Bill of Rights, affirming that every person has:

- The right to determine how they want to die
- The right to name who will have legal and emotional responsibility over their body after death
- The right to choose cremation, embalming, green burial, or donation to science
- The right to a decent burial or cremation—even during war, natural disaster, or hardship
- The right to choose their final resting place

Just because you're gone doesn't mean your wishes disappear. Even in death, your choices deserve to be honored.

Designing a Good Goodbye

Why settle for a somber, conventional funeral when you could have a *Good Goodbye*—a farewell that reflects who you really are?

You might not have been able to control everything in life—your childhood, your health, your job—but you *can* shape your exit. Think of it like a final gathering where you set the tone and the guest list.

Start by asking yourself:

- Who do I want to be there?
- Do I want a quiet memorial, a joyful celebration of life, or something else entirely?
- What do I want done with my body when I'm done using it?
- Is there a location that feels right as a final resting place?
- Who should receive my money, belongings, and sentimental keepsakes?
- Are there people I do *not* want involved in my goodbye?

You don't have to leave these decisions up to chance—or force your loved ones to guess. Creating a plan ahead of time not only gives you peace of mind, but also lifts a huge burden off those you leave behind. They'll be able to let go with more love, less stress, and fewer regrets.

Create Regret-Free Goodbyes

Why wait? You can start today—*not* because you expect to leave soon, but because you want to leave well.

As the old song goes, "I did it my way." Why shouldn't that apply to your farewell too?

By planning your Good Goodbye now, you reduce the risk of conflict, confusion, and grief later. You replace guessing with clarity. You offer your loved ones the gift of knowing they did exactly what you wanted. And you give yourself the chance to write your own final chapter—thoughtfully, beautifully, and in full color.

We may have a few regrets in life—but let's try not to have any when it's time to say goodbye.

2

Going My Way

Going My Way

Who are *you*?

Seriously. Who are you—and how do you want people to remember you?

Do the people in your life really *know* who you are?

Most of us would like to think they do. But let's be honest—many people don't. They may know parts of us. The safe parts. The public parts. But few truly know the full, complex story of who we've been, who we are, and who we still dream of becoming.

We grow, change, shed skins, and carry secret longings. And often, the people around us only ever meet a sliver of our true selves.

The Puzzle of Our Lives

Take Genevive, a kind housekeeper who worked for Max, an older man in his 80s. She cooked and cleaned for him for years, chatting and sharing stories. She knew him as a quiet, gentle man. After he passed, she was asked to help pack up his office. As she removed books from his shelves, she realized with shock that Max had published dozens of influential works and had been a world-renowned expert in his field. She'd heard his name before—but had no idea it belonged to *him*.

He never told her. He didn't think she needed to know. She only saw the side he chose to show her.

The One They'll Never Know

Sometimes, the most profound parts of us remain hidden—even from those we love most.

A woman I know described her life like the main character in The Bridges of Madison County; she had a stable life, a good husband, healthy kids, and a respectable place in the community. But one day she met someone—someone who lit her up from the inside. A deep, impossible kind of love. A love that made her feel alive again. She faced a heart-wrenching choice: abandon her family for a love that thrilled her soul, or stay and honor the life she had built.

She stayed. And no one ever knew. Sometimes when she drifted off in thought, her family would ask what was on her mind. She'd just smile. They didn't know. They never would. She gave up a version of herself for their sake, and they would never know how much she had sacrificed.

When People Get It Wrong

Mama was laid out in an open casket at the funeral home. I'd moved away from my hometown years before, but we spoke nearly every day. I thought I knew her—and that her friends knew about me.

But during visiting hours, a woman I didn't recognize came up to me.

"Who are you?" she asked.

"I'm her daughter," I replied.

Her face hardened. "No, you're not. I was her best friend. She only had a son."

I was stunned. "Well, I *am* her daughter," I said gently.

"You're lying," she snapped. "I don't know who you are—but you're not her daughter."

That moment haunted me. Somehow, someone who claimed to know my mother so well didn't even know I existed. What else about her life had been hidden?

The Thread of a Hidden Life

Emily works at the library. To most people, she's just "the librarian"—quiet, responsible, maybe even a little boring. But that's just the surface. Behind the scenes, Emily's life is layered and fierce. She's a single mom. She's raising a disabled child and supporting another who dreams of being a rock musician. On weekends, she drums in her kid's band—black leather, tattoos, and all. She volunteers at hospice. While her car license plate reads WrldTrvr, she has never fulfilled her dreams of traveling to seeing the world. She can't afford to. At work, she wears long sleeves to cover her ink and a polite smile to meet the expectations of her role. Her coworkers think they know her. "They have no idea," she says.

And she's right. They don't.

Who Will Tell *Your* Story?

Most of us live lives that others only *think* they understand. Even those we love most may only know versions of us that we've filtered, edited, or tucked away. Sometimes that's because we're private. Sometimes it's because we've made sacrifices, endured traumas, or lived quietly in the shadows.

But if you want to be truly remembered—*as you really are*—you need to leave your story behind.

Don't expect people to guess. Tell them. Show them. Write it down.

You are the only person who sees the whole puzzle of your life.

Unless you choose to share it, people will only see scattered pieces—and the image they form may have little to do with the truth.

Who Are You, Really?

In our heart of hearts, many of us go through life without anyone—even our family—*truly* knowing who we are.

As we contemplate our death, we often find ourselves reflecting on the life we've lived.

But here's the truth:

**We can't expect others to know who we are
if we don't even know ourselves.**

So let's go back to the big question:

Who are you—*really*?

Take a quiet moment to consider these:

- What have been your greatest joys?
- What have been your deepest sorrows?
- What do you wish you were?
- What do you wish you weren't?
- What do you wish you had done—but didn't?
- What are you sorry that you *did*?
- What would you do over again in a heartbeat?
- If you could rewrite your life, what would you change?
- What mistakes have you made—and what have they taught you?
- Who has mattered most to you, and why?
- Who do you struggle with or detest—and what, if anything, do you want to do about that?
- What experiences have shaped you that no one else may know about?
- What have you learned that you would like to pass on?
- What do you want people to *know* and *remember* about you? What do you want your legacy to be?

YOU have a lot of control over that!

Imagining the End

Think of this book as your *GoodBye Party and Transformation Guide*. It is designed to help you reflect on your life and prepare for your death in a way that feels meaningful, empowering, and, yes—*liberating*. It will help you make decisions ahead of time so that you can wrap up your life with clarity, confidence, and peace.

Traditionally, funerals have been somber events—people dressed in black, sad music playing, grief heavy in the air. But is *that* how you want your exit to be?

When we think that our time here is coming to a close, we may feel the urge to get our affairs in order. That's not just about paperwork—it's a form of *preliminary grieving* for ourselves. And it's also a chance to prepare others for life after we're gone.

Of course, death is sad. It's the end of something, and someone.

In many traditions, people gather to scatter ashes or place a casket into the ground—symbolic gestures meant to honor a life and support the grieving.

But these rituals don't have to be scripted. They can be *your own*. Later in this book, we'll explore creative and personal ways to say goodbye—ceremonies, letters, video messages, legacy projects.

The way we leave this world *will* shape how people remember us. Most of us want to be remembered with warmth, love, and a sense of meaning.

We May Not Be Famous, But We Matter

Most of us will never win a Nobel Prize or receive the key to the city. But that doesn't mean we haven't left a powerful mark.
Maybe you were the teacher who lit a spark in a child's heart.
Maybe you were the neighbor who always lent a hand.
Maybe you made someone feel loved when they needed it most.
Our small acts of goodness are a "pebble in the pond".
We may have created ripples that continue beyond our view.

There's a saying from India:
Wise people plant trees under whose shade they do not expect to sit.
That's legacy.

Telling the Greatest Story Never Told

By choosing to talk openly about death, you give your loved ones a tremendous gift: clarity, peace, and freedom from regret.

You can model what it looks like to face the inevitable with grace, truth, and courage.

Your goodbye can be someone else's healing.

Think of your life as the *Greatest Story Never Told*.

So go tell it.

Get friendly with yourself before you say goodbye.

As Shakespeare wrote,

"To thine own self be true."

Or in the words of Kahlil Gibran:

"You would know the secret of death. But how shall you find it unless you seek it in the heart of life?"

Cherish the Only You

You've had an amazing life.
You are beautiful.
Your eyes have seen so much.
Your journey has been as unique as your fingerprint.
You are the only "you" that will ever exist.

You are here to shine, even if just for a moment.

So own your light.
Share your story.
Cherish that.
Cherish YOU.

Whether you write it down, record a video, or speak it aloud—let people know who you are. You can tell your clergy, a counselor, or even a stranger if that feels safer than telling your family.

And let's be honest: families can be our toughest audience. Especially the ones who act like they know what's best for us.

You Hold the Pen

You have *so much* influence over your legacy.

You can choose to die with your story untold—or to speak, write, or show people who you truly are.

Pema Chödrön reminds us *How We Live Is How We Die.*

We have a choice about how we spend our energy, our money, our time—and our lives.

We also have choices about how we want to be remembered.

How we say goodbye.

What we do with our body, our money, our land, our "stuff" *can* feel overwhelming.

But I'll help you take it step by step.

A Nourishing Next Chapter

The chapters that follow will offer you food for thought—ideas to digest, chew on, and make your own.

This journey isn't just about dying.

It's about living—*truly* living—until the very end.

And making sure your story echoes long after your voice goes quiet.

3

Death is Relational and Transactional

Death makes one truth painfully clear:

We are defined by our relationships.

As we create our *GoodBye Plan*, the first essential step is to understand this:

We Are Relational Beings

Your death will impact others.

Your relationships—past and present—shape how you feel about life and death. And how you feel about *yourself* shapes everything that follows.

The Most Important Relationship: You with Yourself

Without question, the most important relationship to unpack is your relationship with yourself.

- How well do you know yourself?
- How kind are you to yourself?

- Do you accept yourself, with all your flaws and strengths?
- Who are the people you care most about?
- What do you want to make sure that they understand about who you are and what your life means?

This internal dialogue will frame how you face the final chapter of your life.

The Second Most Important Relationship: You with Those You're Leaving Behind

For most of us, our greatest concern at the end of life is for those we love.

We have shaped our days—and years—around them:

- Parents and children
- Lovers and spouses
- Friends and neighbors
- Coworkers and community groups
- Beloved pets
- People who depend on us
- Dreams and projects still in motion

We don't want to leave them.

We've invested time, love, and energy building these bonds.
They've given us reasons to laugh, cry, grow, and care.
We've created daily rhythms around them:
We wake thinking about them.
We spend our days helping or connecting with them.
We fall asleep hoping for good things for them.
It hurts to imagine saying goodbye.

And deep down, we wonder:
What will they do without us?
Will they miss us?
And carry us in their heart?

We're Needed—and We Need Others

Needing others isn't weakness—it's being human.
Believing that others need us isn't arrogance—**it's love.**

Maybe they need us for:

- Advice
- Protection
- Comfort
- Support
- Partnership
- Laughter
- Companionship
- Financial help

And we need them just as much—for those same reasons.

Loving each other helps us become our best selves.

Life and Death Are Both Transactional

What we say and do *in life* influences how we face our *death*.

When we live with kindness, love, and generosity, we are more likely to face our end with peace instead of despair. Erik Erikson's stages of psycho-social development remind us that the final task of life is to achieve integrity— **Believing that our life had meaning and coherence.**

But it's hard to feel at peace when we're worried—especially about who will take care of the people (and pets) who rely on us.

Who Will Care for the Ones We Love?

Many of us worry deeply about leaving behind:

- Children
- Elderly parents
- Pets
- Vulnerable loved ones

It's a BIG worry. It's normal. It shows up in your heart and in your mind.

Throughout history, people have found unique ways to stay "with" those they love after death.

Stories exist of ancient cultures, like the Egyptians, burying pets with their owners so they could be together in the afterlife. While today that might seem extreme, the underlying sentiment is familiar:

We want to continue caring for those we love, even after we're gone.

Cynthia, for instance, plans to be cremated and buried with the remains of all the deceased pets she has loved throughout her life. "I don't feel right having them dumped just anywhere," she says. "I want to keep them with me forever."

Is that sweet or a little twisted?

It depends on how you look at it. But at its heart, it's about love.

Love makes us want to stay. Randolph and Isabelle were both diagnosed with cancer. They lived much longer than predicted—by years. Their stories aren't rare. Some people outlive terminal diagnoses through grit, hope, or an unwillingness to go just yet. Sometimes, the *will to live* is stronger than medical odds.

Love does that.

Love keeps us here.
Love gives us the will to live
and to give love a chance to live after we are gone.

When we look back on our lives, we'll find joy—and sorrow.
We'll smile about the good times.
We'll cringe at mistakes.
We'll reflect on regrets:

- "I wish I had treated someone better."
- "I should have made a different choice."
- "I regret not caring for my health, education, money, or relationships more wisely."

And that's okay.

Almost everyone has said or done something they regret.
Almost everyone has been a jerk at some point.

What matters most is *not* whether you lived a perfect life.
What matters is what you do *now* with the time you have left.

Whether you forgive yourself.
Whether you seek peace.
Whether you leave behind a story worth telling.
Whether you say what needs to be said

Welcome to the club. Accept the Fact: We've all screwed up.

It is *impossible* to move through life without making mistakes. Some of them are small and easily fixable. Others? Big, painful, and hard to make right. Sometimes we mess up because we didn't know better. Other times, we acted out of anger, fear, or even cruelty. And when that happens—especially if we've hurt someone—we often carry guilt, shame, or regret.

The question is: What are we going to do about it?

The Weight of Regret

Guilt and regret can be heavy loads. For some of us, they don't fade with time. We carry them for years—sometimes decades. The sting of being wronged can last long after the event, especially if we never received the apology we needed.

But here's the hard truth:

There may be people we hurt who are still waiting for our apology, too.

As we age—and especially as we begin to think about our own death—it may be wise to reflect on what we need to make right.
Not just for others, but for *ourselves*.
Forgiveness is powerful.
Forgiving others is hard.

But forgiving ourselves? That's often the hardest of all.

Most of the Time, We Did the Best We Could

There's a big difference between **won't** and **can't**.

If we *could* have helped and *wouldn't*, that's one thing. But if we *wanted* to help and *couldn't*, that's something entirely different.

There are times in life when we're stretched thin—physically, emotionally, and financially. Maybe we were sick. Maybe we were overwhelmed. Maybe we just didn't have the resources, knowledge, or support to do better at the time.

Remember – we live in a world where we often judge others without knowing the full story. This is why it is helpful for you to have the opportunity to be the one who tells your story.

We live in a culture that often jumps to blame. As we go through life, there's times when we may have passed judgment on others – and they have judged us in ways that are not fair. Everyone has a backstory – one we usually don't know.

Being as gentle with ourselves as we would be with someone we love—especially someone who tried and failed—is an act of grace.

Just as we try to give people space, a word of advice to our families and friends - Don't Impose Your Life on ME

It is common for loved ones to "help" us as we tiptoe towards the end of our lives. They may do this without our asking them for help. We may not want their involvement.

But as many people find out, their families march in to take control.

- Of their finances
- Of their healthcare
- Of their diet
- Of their appointments
- Of their transportation
- Of their social life
- Of their recreation
- Of where they live
- Of where they can go

Many of us have boundary issues. This is especially true in families.

They become especially apparent as we near the boundaries between life and death.

Our loved ones may not see what they are doing as a boundary violation. They may not think that they are controlling. That they are stealing our independence – and making us dependent.

If we confront them about being invasive, they may get angry. Their withdrawal of love is something that we do not need towards the end of our lives. There is less time to make up for hurtful interactions that occur.

Stories of Love and Control

Bootsy came down with cancer. She wanted to live in her riverside home where the birds chirped and boats passed by. Her daughter could not bear to let her die. Boots sold her house and moved to a desert area far from waterways to live with her daughter, who was her sole contact in this new land. She went through several difficult surgeries that she didn't want to have because "it will make my girl feel that she did all the right things for me and not have any guilt."

It is not uncommon for people to sacrifice their lives to please their children. It is very common for adult children to push their agendas for how they want their parents to age or die. When they do this, perhaps it is something that you want. Something that will make your life easier or better.

Or it's not something you need or want.

Remember – you have a right to do things your way.

Don't try to steer a ship that isn't yours to captain.

Your life is not their life – and their life is not yours.

Lindy is the mother of a 37-year-old child named Alex. Alex has some social and emotional struggles that interfere with holding jobs and sustaining relationships—but is largely functional. Lindy, however, has convinced herself that Alex could never survive independently. She's made Alex the center of her universe. Lindy has already made a plan: When she nears death, she will gently kill Alex, then kill her beloved cat (whom she believes no one else can care for), and finally take her own life. In Lindy's mind, this is love. In reality, this is fear, control, and a profound violation of boundaries.

Jane's adult children have challenges, too. But Jane has worked hard to give them what they need: education, stability, and skills for life. Her children don't live the lives she dreamed of for them—but she accepts that their lives are *theirs*, not hers. Jane helps when she can, but she doesn't overstep. "I can't always be there for them," she says. "So I need to help them build a life that works without me."

In all these cases, there is deep love. Bootsy gave up her independence to alleviate her daughter's feelings of helplessness and guilt. Jane understands that love doesn't mean control. Lindy's fear of separation has become a prison—for her and for Alex.

It's our job to make the most of this opportunity called *life*.

And yes—it's also part of our job to help others make the most of theirs.

But it is *not* our job to have others live their lives for us.

The issue of boundaries in our relationships show up again and again, often around the giving of money.

Boundary issues often show up in how we give (or withhold) **money.**

Some people spend everything on themselves, believing they earned it and don't owe anyone anything. Others deny themselves pleasure in hopes of leaving something behind for loved ones. Both choices can be valid. But they can also be loaded with unspoken expectations and emotional transactions.

Jason inherited money from his civic-minded parents. He had many ways he could have used it—to donate, to support nieces and nephews, or to build something lasting. Instead, he gave it to his daughter and her reckless son, who spent it on off-road vehicles, gambling, and assault rifles. Jason disapproved—but he did it anyway. Why? Because he was desperate for his daughter's love. And he feared that saying no would mean losing it. He died with his inheritance being a poor investment instead of helping the causes he said he loved.

Ted was a college librarian who lived simply, drove an old car, and wore the same set of clothes for years. When he died, he left a multi-million dollar estate to the university to help struggling students. Because he had not specified how the money was to be used, the college purchased a big, glitzy scoreboard for the football team.

It is a reminder to Ted and to Jason's parents to specify exactly what they want to happen with the money they leave behind. Otherwise, those in charge may make self-serving decisions about where it goes.

Our Relationship Doesn't Die When We Do

Just because the body is gone doesn't mean the relationship is over. Our presence echoes long after we're buried.

- **Tony** lights candles and says prayers for his grandmother every year on the anniversary of her death.
- **Windsong** performs seasonal rituals to honor her ancestors and ask for their protection.
- **Lucianna** teaches her children to cook family recipes, passed down from generations of women before her.

These are more than traditions. They are acts of remembrance, continuity, and spiritual connection.

Corina had a father who was unkind to her for most of her life. When he died, he left her enough money to buy a home, go to college, or start a business. In doing so, he became—finally—the kind of father she had always needed. It didn't erase the pain, but it helped. It was a gesture of healing. And it worked, for both of them.

We Carry Our Ancestors—Literally

There is a whole body of research about epigenetics that proves how what happens in one generation gets passed on to future ones, not just in how we look but in how we act and how we feel. In the book, *Matrescence: The Cellular Science of the Unself*, Lucy Jones writes that we carry within our genetic structure all the family members who came before us. Their physical, emotional, and spiritual imprints are embedded in our cells. We are not just shaped by their love or trauma—we are, in some ways, made of them.

Life and death aren't just personal experiences.

They are intergenerational transactions—with our past and our future.

We love. We worry. We mold our lives around others.

As we think about death being relational and transactional, consider the following:

- We don't want to die if it means losing those relationships.
- Death is loss but it can also be transformed into a gift.
- Death brings grief, frustration, sadness—and sometimes, quiet relief.
- When we don't have healthy boundaries in life, our death can create *more pain* for the people we leave behind.
- What regrets or unresolved relationships still weigh on me?
- Have I ever judged someone unfairly without knowing their full story?
- Where have I confused "can't" with "won't"—in myself or in others?

- Is there anyone I need to forgive? Is there anyone I hope will forgive me?
- What do I need to accept in order to release guilt or regrets I've been carrying?

We want to think about how our actions and emotions get intertwined with those of others. It is important to approach death with as much awareness, intention, love, and peace as possible.

We are connected.
Now and forever.

4

The Disclosure Dilemma

D*isclosure*

Who Gets to Know We're Dying?

Let's turn to a touchy subject.

If you think your time has few days again, do you want to tell anyone? Or do you want to keep this private matter to yourself?
 is a big question that has big implications for the rest of your life.

Dying is a process—a slow, uneven descent. It rarely happens all at once.

**Instead, it unfolds in stages, spits, and fits—
sometimes with warning, sometimes without.**

HOW DO WE KNOW WE ARE DYING?

We might find out from a doctor.
We might not hear it said out loud—but know it in our bones.
Our body may whisper it, then shout, then break down.
We may have no idea it is coming until it arrives.
Dying is a usually a process.

A confusing one.

Our cells are always dying and rebuilding.
Our lives are always full of endings and new beginnings.

It's hard to know when the end times are coming.

The signs of our time growing shorter are often subtle - at first:

- Grey hair
- Wrinkled or tissue-paper like skin
- Balding
- Wearing glasses because we can't see squat without them
- Slower walking, shorter distances
- Liver spots that mark the passage of time
- Trouble with mobility—stairs, distances, dropped items, fear of falling
- Lumps and bumps we pretend not to notice
- Turning up the volume on the TV and still missing the words
- Being accused of forgetfulness
- Needing more time to do what we once did without a second thought

These are reminders—gentle or blunt—that our bodies are winding down.

The Question of Knowing influences the way we view ourselves and our relationships, and our future.

If we had an inkling that our time was limited—
Would we say it out loud?

Would we tell the people we love?
Would we even admit it to ourselves?
Some people know and prepare.
Others know, but pretend they don't.
And some never see it coming at all.

This leaves us with The Disclosure Dilemma.

As the truth of our mortality sets in, many of us face a tough decision:
Who do we tell?
What do we tell them?
And what do we want from them in return?

Some of us feel compelled to share our truth.
Others hold it close, fearing pity, panic, or loss of control.
There is no one right answer.

Choosing when and how to talk about dying can be an act of personal choice.

Different Choices, Different Endings

Harry knew something was wrong. The lump on her back. The missed appointments. The growing forgetfulness. But Harry had always been a bit scattered, so others chalked it up to "just being Harry." Did she know she was dying? Probably. Did she tell anyone? Not a soul. Harry believed her dying was her business. She wanted to live as normally as possible, for as long as she could.

Walt, by contrast, was open about his decline. He had beaten cancer twice and lived a long, rich life. At 94, he knew the end was near—and everyone knew it too. He talked with his family about his wishes. When his time came, he passed peacefully in a beautiful hospice surrounded by the people (and dogs!) he loved. Flowers, music, memories—it was everything he wanted. Walt gave his family the gift of closure and clarity.

When it comes to disclosure, medical professionals often walk a fine line.

They want patients to have support, but they're bound by privacy laws like HIPAA. They can't tell family members unless they have written permission. It's not their business.

That's why things like Living Wills, healthcare proxies, and advance directives are so important. These documents speak for us when we can't speak for ourselves. They tell doctors whether to keep us alive at all costs—or let us go gently.

Without them, doctors may default to family members, who may not always know—or honor—our wishes.

When Dignity Means Deciding

Jim Mac knew what was coming. Dementia ran in his family, and the signs had started. He didn't want to end up institutionalized, a body to be "toileted, fed, and done to." With help from his doctors and loved ones, Jim made a courageous decision to leave on his own terms. His family grieved, but they also celebrated his life—and respected the way he chose to exit it.

When you plan ahead, everyone benefits. They know what to expect. It gives us all time to put things into order and to have the communications that facilitate our going forward.

This is unlike what happens when you don't make a plan and don't tell others what you want. Consider the next story about what happened to Tanya and The Unspoken Risks of Silence.

Tanya had a minor stroke that should have been a wake-up call. She made some changes—improved her diet, exercised more. But a major stroke soon followed. This time, it left her speechless, motionless, and dependent on others for everything. Though she had a will, she hadn't anticipated this kind of ending. The people she distrusted—her "no-good" family—took over. They controlled her care, her money, her belongings, and her relationships. Trapped inside her body, Tanya became both a medical prisoner and a personal one.

Whether or not we disclose our dying process is one of the last significant choices we have. It's a decision about:

- Control
- Privacy
- Protection
- And sometimes, love

Sometimes telling others helps them prepare.
Sometimes it protects us from unwanted interference.
And sometimes, we don't know what to say, or how to say it..
When possible, naming our wishes—and documenting them—is a gift we give to ourselves and those who may have to carry us to the end.

To choose or Not to Choose – That is the Question.

Beth knew she was dying. She had thoughts about what she wanted—and didn't want—but she wouldn't speak up. As a child, she learned to survive by doing what others expected of her. That training became her default: go along to get along. Don't rock the boat. Keep quiet.

After her husband died, her oldest son, Jasper, stepped in. He took control of her checkbook and her legal decisions. He rewrote her will, giving himself power over her and her assets. Then he put the paper in front of her and handed her the pen.

"I don't agree with what Jasper is doing," Beth whispered once. "But I don't want him mad at me."

She didn't feel strong enough to fight. It was easier to let it all slide—her power, her voice, her legacy. Jasper took everything of value, leaving scraps for the other children and grandchildren to argue over.

Beth's story was never told—at least, not by her.

How Many of Us Are Like Beth?

Afraid to speak.
Afraid to be disliked, disrespected, or retaliated against.
Afraid that if we speak our truth, we'll be punished for it.
When we lack support or feel vulnerable, it can be easier to give in to manipulators than to stand up to them.
And that's completely human.
Sometimes, not saying we're sick or dying—or what we want when we go—is a form of self-protection.
Sometimes silence feels safer than the fallout of honesty.
But what do we lose in that silence?

We often don't tell the truth the whole truth and nothing but the truth.

Not because we're dishonest—
But because we're afraid we won't be heard,

respected,
or loved.

Ask Yourself:

- Who do you trust enough to tell your truth?
- If you were to confide your story—your hopes, fears, and final wishes—who would you choose?
- Who's the last person you'd want to know?
- If you do share that you're dying, what do you hope to receive? Comfort? Support? Understanding?
- And what are you afraid might happen? Rejection? Control? Disregard?
- If you don't tell anyone what you want, are you okay with others deciding everything for you?

These are not easy questions. But they are necessary ones.

Telling—or Not Telling—Has Consequences

Here's a simple way to weigh both sides:

Pros of Telling	Cons of Telling
Support and assistance	Interference and manipulation
Opportunity to reconcile	Emotional turbulence in others
Clarity about your wishes	Power struggles and conflict
Time to put affairs in order	Family infighting

Some people, like Walt and Jim Mac, chose to share openly that their time was near. Their families responded with love and support, putting their own egos aside to honor the final requests of someone they loved deeply. They died with dignity and peace. If there is such a thing as a happy death, theirs came close.

Others, like Beth and Harry, knew what was coming—but stayed quiet. They feared what would happen if they spoke up, and unfortunately, what they feared came true.

Families dictated:

- Where she lived
- What she wore
- What she ate
- When she could use the toilet
- Who she could see
- What happened to her money

Many people become prisoners in their own life. Tanya lay in bed, waiting for the good Lord to take her—while others controlled everything else.

Is That the Way You Want to Go?
Or...
What About Doing It Your Way?

What would it look like to speak your truth?
To write down your wishes?
To choose who gets a say—and who doesn't?

Your choices matter.

Your life—and your death—belong to you.
But only if you claim them.

Disclosing That You're Dying: The Gift and the Gamble

Disclosing that you're dying can be a simple, supportive act.

It lets others know you care about them—and it opens the door for them to tell you that you matter to them.

Done well, it can become part of a peaceful, meaningful send-off.

But let's be honest:

Sometimes telling others that you're dying can backfire.

You may know, deep down, that saying it out loud will unleash a storm—and bring on hell on earth long before you've left it.

Telling is a Gamble—So Bet on What Feels Right

Disclosing that you're dying is a risk—just like living.

There's no one-size-fits-all approach.

But if you trust yourself to tell the right people, in the right way, at the right time, it can be one of the most liberating and empowering acts of your life.

As Tim McGraw recommends - Live like you were dying.

It is important that we make the most of each day.

Relish the moments.

Tell your truth to yourself, even if not to others.

And put your life in order—not just for others, but for you.

Because when you face dying with thoughtfulness, intention, and grace,

you create not only a better goodbye—

You create a better life right up to the end.

5

The Life Review

The Life Review

"I had the time of my life"

Conducting a Life Review can happen at any point in our lives, but it often becomes especially meaningful when we sense our days are numbered. It's closely tied to the topic of disclosure from the last chapter. Reviewing our lives stirs up memories, highlights successes, surfaces regrets, and often calls forth secrets that long to be told—or laid to rest.

MEMORIES

If you're anything like me, your mind sometimes catapults into the past without warning.
Maybe you'll be washing dishes and suddenly recall a conversation from years ago.
Some memories seem to visit us regularly. Others sneak up on us when we least expect them.

But why do some memories stick while others fade?

Psychologists tell us that memories emerge to help us navigate the present.

When we face something today that echoes a past event, our brains dive into the archive for something that might guide us.

Some memories offer comfort and sweetness—others remind us of pain and loss, or lessons still unresolved.

As we do a Life Review, we make room for both.

When we're focusing on creating a *Good Goodbye*, let's first choose to dwell in the **positive**—the moments that made our lives feel rich, joyful, and alive.

Here are a few memory prompts to stir your heart:

- Your first kiss
- The first time your body felt *fireworks*
- The smell of fresh-baked cookies... or someone's cologne
- A night laughing with friends until your belly hurt
- A song that takes you back in time
- That deep pride from accomplishing something hard
- A moment of déjà vu—feeling like you've *been here before*

Our memories are uniquely ours. Some repeat themselves in our minds like looping songs—maybe to teach us something, maybe just to bring comfort.

What are the memories that show up for *you* again and again?

What are the stories you want to make sure others know before you go?

REMEMBERING OUT LOUD

Sharing memories can be a gift—to yourself, and to those you leave behind.

They offer insight into who you are, what you valued, and what shaped you.

You might want to reflect on:

- **Your favorite memories** you'd like others to know about
- **Stories, yours and those handed to you by others**
- **Moments of joy, triumph, or silliness** that capture your spirit
- **People who meant the most to you,** and why
- **Times you felt deeply loved—or deeply loving**

We'll get into your **successes**, **regrets**, and **secrets** next—three core areas that shape any Life Review.

But first, pause.

Let your memories surface.

Take a breath, maybe even close your eyes, and see what comes to mind.

Remembering isn't just about looking back.
It's about discovering what still matters, even now.

SUCCESS

There's **a lot of pressure** on us to be successful.

Too much pressure, if you ask me.

On any given day, we might feel like a failure simply because we didn't measure up to someone else's definition of success. Sometimes we fret because someone we barely know passed judgment on us. Someone that doesn't know our story, or challenges, or how hard we have worked. And that's just plain **dumb**.

So let's reframe the question:

What do *you* think your greatest successes have been?

Success Comes in All Types and Sizes

We often assume that success has to be something big—a headline, a promotion, a gold medal. But real success doesn't have to be flashy. Even the smallest actions can ripple forward and matter deeply.

Think of the tiny blossom that feeds the tiny bee, who makes the sweet honey that sweetens your tea. That's success.

In fact, just surviving another **day** is often a success in itself.

"Any day you wake up on this side of the dirt is a good day," according to Kyle.

"Every day affords us a miracle to make miracles," says Audrey.

"I wake up every morning creating a plan for what I'm going to do today to help others and to make it a happy day," —Christy.

Success means different things at different times.

What being successful means to you at age 10 isn't the same as at 25, 45, or 80.

Our **health**, our **work**, our **relationships**, and where we live all play into how we measure success—and sometimes just *keeping going* is the most impressive victory of all.

My Hand and the Coffee Cup

Not long ago, I had an accident that left my right arm paralyzed—shoulder to fingertip. I couldn't move a thing. I was terrified that I was never going to be able to move my hand or arm again. This paralysis lasted for months, and I was so sad and scared. An occupational therapist worked with me using different techniques.. And then, one day, my little finger twitched. It moved just a bit. This was **huge**! After months of daily exercises and relentless practice, I eventually managed to lift all five fingers a half-inch off the table. Later, I poured a cup of coffee with one hand. I could pick it up and put it to my mouth. Not a big deal for most people—but for me, it felt like a **miracle**.

That's success.

Success Wears Many Faces

- Marvin died peacefully, surrounded by love. He had climbed the ladder in his career, earned professional honors, and created a home full of warmth and gardens. When he passed, the community turned out in droves to celebrate his life.
- Max won a Nobel Prize.
- Trudy had a street named after her.
- Tom built a little table that didn't fall down.
- Meme learned how to do a somersault.
- Stephen published 42 books.
- Mindy published an essay in the school newspaper.
- Rachel became a TV star.

- Tony graduated high school.
- Mary finally made sourdough bread that *rose*.
- Mike made a hit record.
- Bo did 25 push-ups.
- Marty signed up for a 5K.
- Tiny passed the driving test.

Big or small, these moments matter.
They're all successes.

What Is *Your* Definition of Success?

Now it's your turn.
Forget what society, your job, or even your family might say.

What are the things that *you* feel proud of?
Here are some prompts to help you reflect:

- **Successes in school** (elementary, high school, college, or informal learning)
- **Success at work**, whether as an employee, entrepreneur, or caregiver
- **Success with your body** (recovery, fitness, health improvements)
- **Relationship wins** (building or healing bonds with friends, family, partners—even pets)
- **Accomplishments you've kept to yourself**, but that mean a lot
- **Overcoming a fear**, a habit, or an emotional hurdle
- **Facing your demons—and not letting them win**

Sometimes we forget all the things we have accomplished in our life. Big or small, take time to remember them.

Celebrate Yourself

In a world full of critics and unrealistic expectations, take time to **honor the victories** you've earned.

Each day, try to name one thing you did well. And as you reflect on your life's journey—especially as the autumn years unfold—pause to admire the **full sweep of your accomplishments**.

Big or small, they're yours. They matter. And they tell the story of a life well-lived.

REGRETS

Everyone has regrets.

Things we said that we wish we hadn't.
Things we didn't say but wish we had.
Actions we took that we wish we could undo.
Opportunities we missed or choices we didn't make.
Decisions made too quickly or without enough thought.
Intentions that were good but whose outcomes weren't.

The list is endless. We blame and shame ourselves. We beg for a do-over. We wish we could turn back time.

But we can't. Living with that is hard. And self-defeating.

What is THE MOST HEART-WRENCHING and PAINFUL REGRET?

Not telling people that we love them, that we're proud of them, that they matter to us.

As we wrap up the story of our life for ourselves, and for others, here is a list of common regrets.

DO YOU RECOGNIZE YOURSELF IN ANY OF THEM?

Romantic Relationships

- I regret choosing the wrong partner.
- I stayed too long when I should have left.
- I'm sorry I let someone special go.
- I regret that someone special let me go.
- I cared too much and put too much pressure on them.
- I didn't cherish them enough.
- I didn't give the relationship a fair chance.
- I regret not apologizing, or not really meaning it when I did.
- I wish I'd expressed my needs or feelings clearly.
- I overlooked their background or health struggles.
- I made excuses for their bad behavior (laziness, substance use, infidelity, violence).
- I endured domestic violence hoping things would improve.
- I didn't stand up for myself or my boundaries.
- I lost myself and feel sorry about that.
- I didn't communicate or listen very well.
- I made assumptions without knowing the truth.
- I gave everything and felt unappreciated—there's resentment.

Friendships and Peers

- I regret that I didn't take time to build friendships.
- I am sorry that I was part of a certain group or clique.
- I wish I had stood up to a bully.
- I regret not listening to wise advice about who to avoid.
- I regret losing touch with important people.
- I wish I had played or had more fun.
- I regret judging someone unfairly.
- I wish I had listened more and talked less.
- I cared too much about what others thought of me.
- I regret not helping friends when they needed me.
- I wish I had been more genuine or honest.
- I regret gossiping or speaking poorly about others.
- I wish I'd focused more on pleasing myself, not others.
- I regret buying into superficial things (clothes, tattoos, haircuts) to "fit in."
- I didn't treat myself with the kindness I give others.
- I regret seeking approval instead of self-love.
- I regret not visiting loved ones before they died.

Physical and Mental Health

- I wish I hadn't wasted time worrying so much.
- I regret not seeking counseling sooner.
- I wish I had exercised more regularly.
- I let appearance influence poor health choices.
- I wish I had more confidence in myself.
- I regret not embracing my own unique beauty and intelligence.
- I regret not following medical advice (medications, surgeries).
- I wish I had eaten healthier.
- I regret avoiding doctors or delaying care.

- I relied on false or misleading health information.
- I didn't understand the long-term effects of trauma.
- I wish I had stuck with my physical therapy.
- I regret wearing uncomfortable but fashionable shoes.
- I regret ingesting substances that I knew weren't good for me.
- I am sorry that I didn't get annual check-ups.

Education

- I wish I had worked harder in school.
- I thought being a star athlete would earn me a scholarship, but it didn't.
- I regret not taking grades seriously.
- I wish I had studied subjects I was curious about.
- I regret choosing a school based on others' opinions or finances rather than my heart.
- I missed out on the traditional college experience (like living in dorms).
- I regret not finishing my degree.
- I regret cheating instead of doing my own work.
- I regret the debt I accumulated.
- I regret not traveling and learning about the world more.
- I wish I had majored in a different field of study.
- I regret not taking advantage of opportunities that were available.
- I regret not asking more questions.

Money

- I regret never learning how to manage money well.

- I didn't pay attention to my spending and now I'm paying the price.
- I wish I had saved more.
- I regret getting into debt.
- I regret certain big purchases or missed investments.
- I know I made some poor financial choices.
- I lent money to people who never paid me back.
- I let money control my decisions and relationships.
- I wasted money on things that only temporarily made me feel better.
- I regret falling for scams.

Career

- I regret spending too much time at work and too little at home.
- I prioritized work over important relationships.
- Even when I was home, I was emotionally unavailable because of work stress.
- I stayed in jobs I didn't like just for the paycheck.
- I endured toxic supervisors instead of seeking change.
- I chose jobs or education paths to please others, not myself.

Parenting and Family Relationships

- I regret not listening closely to what my children said.
- I'm sorry I missed meaningful events because I was "too busy."
- I regret yelling and not modeling healthy conflict resolution.
- I regret teaching my children that violence and saying mean things about other people was okay.
- I regret being so overwhelmed that I didn't pay enough attention to you or the things that mattered.

- I wish I had realized how quickly childhood passes—it's gone forever.
- I regret not laughing and finding joy with them more often.
- I'm sorry I didn't protect them from hurtful people quickly enough.
- I regret not spending enough time playing and being outdoors with them.
- I treated family members unequally instead of cherishing each for who they are.
- I regret relying too much on screens and technology instead of encouraging creative play.

How Many Regrets Did You Find?

This list includes **around 60 specific regrets** that cover major life areas: relationships, friendships, health, education, money, career, and parenting. This shows that regrets are *many* and *diverse*—and almost everyone carries quite a few.

Regrets are a natural part of life — a reflection of our humanity and our desire to do better.

Recognizing regrets is an opportunity to learn, to forgive ourselves, and to live the days ahead with intention and compassion.

What Are We Going to Do About Them?

Beating ourselves up for things that we wish we had done differently is of no value. Card laid, card played. We can't change the past, no matter how often or intensely we think about it.

- It's probably **unwise to carry regrets into our grave** without trying to address them.
- Some regrets are **small and fixable**, like a quick apology or a changed behavior.
- Others are **deep and long-lasting**, sometimes held for decades—even a lifetime.
- Holding onto regrets too long can consume us emotionally, sometimes until very old age.
- Near the end of life, people often want to say or hear certain things — love, pride, forgiveness.
- But some regrets **cannot be undone**, no matter how many apologies we make.
- Whether others forgive or let us off the hook depends on the person and family dynamics.
- Some people offer **unconditional love**, washing away our mistakes like waves on a beach.
- Others may **hold onto our flaws and use them as weapons**, unwilling to forgive.
- Recognizing this, we do what we can: **say sorry, seek restorative justice, and try to move on.**
- If forgiveness isn't granted, that reflects more on them than on us.
- Ultimately, **we have to "let it go"** — as the song from *Frozen* says — as best we can.

SECRETS

Everybody Has Secrets. What's Yours?

Most of us carry parts of our past that nobody else knows about.

The question is—**do you want anyone else to know?**

Maybe you've done acts of kindness and generosity you never mentioned. Maybe you've had moments of embarrassment, secret lovers or flings, quiet pregnancies, acts of violence, lies, or protections you shouldn't have made. Maybe you've struggled with suicidal thoughts, drug use, theft, or even crimes. Some of these might seem small and unworthy of sharing; others so big they've stayed locked inside, hush-hush. You might wish to take those secrets to your grave or beyond. Or maybe, as you approach your final goodbye, you want to finally let others see the real you.

Sharing secrets can bond us together – like people working together to create a surprise party for someone, building or buying together that you know someone would really like, or building a bond together.

Sometimes secrets are destructive if people find out that you've kept something from them. This is a big deal with relationships that mean the most to us, like in our family, our friend network, or at work. Secrets can create divisions, "us and them", seem to play favorites, leave people out, estrange others, hurt people, or betray them in some way.

Common secrets include:

- Snooping by looking at what they have on their phone, computer, or social media accounts
- Reading other people's letters, diaries, or personal information
- Going through another person's private property
- Not telling when someone has broken the law or violated a trust

Secrets are kept confidential because we fear that we, or someone else, could get into trouble. Sometimes they are time-limited, and it would be helpful for others to know the truth. Other times, divulging secret information may hurt you or others.

Some secrets are big. And some are not.

Some are worth sharing. And others should never be shared.

IT'S YOUR CHOICE

About whether you want to tell.

As my friend Dave says, *"You always have to tell the truth—but you don't always have to tell all of it."*

Or you might choose to tell only part of it.

Reality is arbitrary, as sociologist Peter Berger suggests.

So, what spin will you put on your secret life?

As the end of our days approaches, we get to choose the story we want to tell, how we tell it, and which pieces to include—or leave out.

Stories From the Edge

When Henry arrived at the funeral home, his mom and sisters were already there, grieving the death of his father. But then Henry noticed something startling: at one end of the coffin stood his family, and at the other end, a woman with children crying their eyes out. It turned out his father had a secret second family—another wife and another set of children—living in the same town, but none of them knew about each other until he died. It was a tense scene, with both families making funeral arrangements. The grief was real, but so was the anger—both sets of children and wives said if their dad wasn't already dead, they might have killed him.

Janice's life held a secret. Years ago, she caused a car accident that killed a man. She was never prosecuted, but the guilt stayed with her. She'd also had an affair with a married man and given up the child for a closed adoption. Later, she married and had two children – none who never knew she was, in her own words, "a murderer," or that they had a brother they'd never meet. She told me all this because she trusted me, and because she didn't want to go to her grave without confessing. I've kept her secret—but wondered if her children would compassionately benefit from knowing the unseen side of their mother – or see her as bad.

Robert holds a secret he's itching to reveal once a certain politician dies. It's a scandal involving cross-dressing and kinky sex that would ruin his rival's career. "I won't say anything now," Robert said, "because the backlash would be fierce. But I'll laugh when his supporters find out."

Marty fell in love with someone, though the feeling was never openly acknowledged. Complicated relationships and circumstances resulted in their keeping their feelings for each other a secret. Now, years later, Marty wonders if keeping that secret was worth it. The silence has only caused regret.

THE LIFE REVIEW IS FOR YOU, not for other people.

It will help you to have a perspective on your life.

It will give you time to fix things that may have haunted you.

It will give you the opportunity to pat yourself on the back and be proud of all you have accomplished, big and small.

Conducting your life review will help you to craft your going away celebration so people can get to know the real you.

Or the you that you want them to remember.

6

Emotions and the Transactional Nature of Death

Death is a process.

Grief is a process too.

>Both unfold slowly, often without clear stages or neat endings.
>It's the unwinding of time.
>The unraveling of love, confusion, longing, and regret.
>We are passengers on a journey into an uncharted abyss—sometimes led gently, sometimes thrown in without warning.

>*Grief continues to evolve.*
>*Anger long stuffed may arise.*

Death changes the way we relate to not just those who have passed over, but also to those who are living.

>*Let's look at how emotions change us – and our relationships.*

There is an Emotional Earthquake of Death

Death unearths emotions we may never have realized we carried.

They may surge the moment we're told we're dying.

They may surface unexpectedly after someone close to us passes.

We may feel profound love one moment, then plummet into rage or despair the next.

Grief can feel like a roller coaster—sudden drops, sharp turns, breathless heights, and chaotic descents.

At times, we might brace ourselves so tightly that we forget to breathe.

Other times, we're flung into emotional territory with no seatbelt.

No matter how well defended you may think you are, everybody is going to get caught in death's emotional web.

Death is a sacred and unsettling journey.

Death is the ultimate journey that we are all going to take. We like to know where we are going, but in this journey, we don't.

Some spiritual traditions offer roadmaps for this passage.

- Buddhism teaches that the soul takes 49 days to transition fully, lingering in a realm between death and rebirth.
- Christianity tells of Jesus rising after three days.
- Other belief systems say 11 days, or 7, or none at all.
- Some believe that restless spirits remain behind—ghosts tethered to unfinished business.
- Others believe that when it's over, it's simply over.

Some people believe in a heaven or a hell.

Others feel that there is a holding zone that occurs between this world and the next.

We will find out when our time arrives.

Having some sort of philosophical, scientific, or spiritual belief system can smooth out the edges as we contemplate "what's next".

Death Is a Transformation

When we die, we give up one kind of presence as we shift into another.

We leave behind memories, unresolved words, unfinished love, and often—unfinished pain.

The people we leave behind inherit not only our money or possessions—

but also our emotional legacy.

The First Law of Thermodynamics states that neither matter nor energy can be **created or destroyed**.

Energy, including life in all of its forms, merely changes.

How this works with souls remains to be seen.

What we do know is that our responses to our own death—and those of others—are shaped by relationship, timing, culture, and unspoken expectations.

> The two major emotions that impact our relationships are Grief and Anger.

Before it happens - We all Must Grieve Our Own Death

When we are the ones who are dying, we grieve the gradual loss of everything familiar:

- Our body
- Our home
- Our identity
- Our loved ones
- Our life as we know it

Grief and the Journey of Dying

Make no mistake: when someone dies, it is deeply sad. Grief can be overwhelming, all-consuming, and devastating. Some of us mask it with a stiff upper lip and say, "I'm fine." Others may collapse to the ground, screaming in agony, curled in a fetal position, unable to get up. Most of us wobble somewhere in between—some days functional, other days unable to get out of bed or even put on our shoes to move forward.

While anger is often an outward expression of our sadness, grief is an internal experience. When we lash out in anger, we want others to feel our pain or know we're upset. But grief is more private—a silent heartbreak we mostly keep to ourselves. Even when we share moments of grief, others only glimpse fragments of our sorrow.

Anger is public; grief is private.

Grief comes in waves—sometimes crashing over us so powerfully we feel swept out to sea. At other times, we seem to float serenely, only to suddenly find ourselves struggling to keep our heads above water.

How we face our imminent departure shapes how those we love will grieve our passing. We are deeply interconnected: your experience influences mine, and mine shapes yours. In this way, grief is transactional.

If we can come to terms with ourselves as we die, we can help those we love grieve more healthily. Grief is natural and necessary—it helps us process loss. How we grieve can either lead to shorter, more constructive healing or prolong pain and damage.

Anticipatory Grief and the Gift of Time

Knowing death is near brings anticipatory grief. Except in sudden, unexpected deaths, most of us die gradually. This slow slide gives us a chance to reflect on life, make amends, and say what needs saying. It allows us to prepare ourselves and those we care about.

As I write this, my 19-year-old tortoiseshell ragdoll cat, Claudia, is nearing the end of her life. She is frail and thin; she struggles to jump on the bed, yet she still enjoys food, drinks water, curling up in the sun, and she purrs as we cuddle. She seems peaceful and not in pain. I'm preparing myself emotionally for when she's ready to let go—and that preparation helps me manage the grief to come.

Eric's Story:
Eric knew he was dying. He gathered the people most important to him and told them so. He expressed his love, gratitude, and blessings. They wept together. Before they left, Eric shared his wishes for his death and funeral. A friend teased him for wanting to control everything, lightening the mood. Laughter followed, questions were asked, and in openly processing his grief, Eric helped his loved ones face theirs. The bonds forged in life grew even stronger through this shared experience, providing support for after he was gone.

Max's Story:
Max had made many mistakes. Selfish and narcissistic in his youth, he hurt others without care. But as he aged and became vulnerable, guilt and regret overwhelmed him. He sought to make amends—donating generously to charities and reaching out personally to those he had wronged. These efforts didn't erase the past but brought healing both to him and those he had harmed.

Grieving the Death of Others

When someone we love dies, our grief depends on the kind of relationship we had with them. This is why it is important to heal rifts while we are alive.

Our grief is also related to the *how* and *when* of their departure.

If death comes suddenly—by accident or tragedy—our grief may come in tidal waves. We may feel robbed, disoriented, and lost.

With no chance to say goodbye.

If the death follows a long illness, the grieving often starts before the person dies. We may mourn the person as they fade. We may feel guilty for hoping their suffering ends. We may have time to plan, to talk, to make peace. Or we may avoid those conversations entirely, out of fear.

Our response to death is relational.

Parents and children grieve when either of them dies – this is the most impactful relationship in our lives. The grief and loneliness may feel overwhelming. We know that our grandparents will pass so while we will miss them, their dying has a context that makes our acceptance of it a bit easier. Many of us have animal family members and they are truly our best friends, so when they pass away, our grief is intense - and may not be understood by non-animal lovers.

The passing of our partner or spouse can be complex indeed. For people who have been together for a long time and grown to really bond with each other, grief is a lot more intense than for partners who have been together a short time, or with whom there has been a conflictual relationship. For those people who sometimes said "I wish you were dead", this dream came true but may leave them with guilt and nightmares instead of relief.

Each death—and each relationship to it—creates a unique emotional map.

Don't *have* an expectation of how grief is going to manifest for you.

There is no right or wrong way to grieve.

People tend to give advice but go back to the theme of this book – *be gentle with yourself and do things your way.*

Taking responsibility for the rough patches in our lives and working to smooth them can ease grief for ourselves and others.
In fact, pre-loss grief—the sorrow felt before someone dies—can sometimes be harder to bear than grief after they are gone.

Grace reflected on the death of someone she loved. "It hurt everyday to watch my beloved die. I felt hopeless and helpless. I struggled to do all I could to make them comfortable and to postpone the inevitable. After they died, curiously it was a sense of relief, both for them and for me. My before-death grief for them was much worse than my grief afterwards".

Caring for Someone Who Is Dying: The Hidden Burden

Caring for a loved one who is dying can be physically, emotionally, and financially exhausting.

You feel like you're there all the time, watching every moment.

Others may not provide the same level of care you would, but as your loved one's needs grow, you want to help even more—while your own needs take a backseat.

The rest of the family needs and wants you too, but you may not have the emotional or physical energy to be fully present for them.

There's a group of people called "the sandwich generation" who are trying to build their own families at the same time they are also trying to care for their aging parents. They do not have enough bandwidth to do it all well and still have a little time for themselves. It's not the of love – it is the lack of time, money, and energy to manage the **care of others.**

If you're trying to work or keep a business afloat during this time, the burden multiplies. Many people end up quitting or "retiring" early just to be able to stay home and care for their loved one. When the person dies, relief is common—not because losing them is easier, but because the overwhelming physical, emotional, social, and financial burdens on the caregiver finally lift. As Lexis said, "It's not better—but it is easier."

Rodney's Story:
Rodney's cancer ravaged his body, and the treatments made him terribly sick. This wasn't living. He didn't want to die, but he certainly

didn't want to live trapped in hospitals, poked and prodded, hooked to tubes, surrounded by strangers, stuck in a painful waiting game.

Betty's Story:
After a stroke left Betty paralyzed except for one hand, she became dependent on others for the most basic needs. She asked the nurse to change her diaper, but the nurse was busy and didn't come for hours. Betty's hand became soiled from trying to clean herself. Eating with the same hand, she picked up e coli. She developed painful bedsores where no one had washed her properly. She feared one nurse in particular, who denied Betty's allegation of abuse. When Betty died, her niece said, "It was a blessing."

Understanding Grief: Kubler-Ross and Beyond

When people think about grief, they often refer to the work of Dr. Elizabeth Kubler-Ross. She brought the topic of grief and dying into public awareness by identifying stages people often go through when facing death:

1. Shock
2. Denial
3. Anger
4. Bargaining
5. Depression
6. Acceptance

Her work helped us understand that grief is normal, takes time, and that people eventually come to accept death as a part of life's cycle.

While this model is classic in the field, it isn't linear and can take different forms for different people.

So don't automatically assume that this is the way grief works.

For you, it could have a different trajectory...

When Grief Becomes Difficult

Not everyone handles grief well. Ideally, pain is intense at first but softens over time.

It helps when we create a narrative that makes sense of the loss—a way to find meaning or acceptance.

If we don't create a positive goodbye, others may struggle more.

While a good exit plan doesn't guarantee easier grief for those left behind, it increases the odds that they will cope better.

Some people experience complicated grief—also called protracted, maladaptive, or "grief spirals"—where the pain lasts longer and disrupts life in harmful ways.

When grief is unresolved, it can morph into different forms – and create a variety of dysfunctional consequences for us.

The Consequences of Complicated Grief

Complicated grief can lead to serious problems:

- **Divorce**
- **Job loss**
- **Physical illness**
- **Substance abuse**
- **Overeating or loss of appetite**
- **Insomnia or excessive sleeping**
- **Major lethargy**
- **Anger and emotional instability**
- **Clinginess or isolation**

Consider these stories:

Terry and Jenny's Story:
Terry and Jenny hadn't been married long. They shared a home and loved their dogs. Terry adored his dog, Missy P, who was inseparable from him. One afternoon, while roughhousing, Jenny's dog Rufus landed and accidentally broke Missy P's neck. Terry was devastated. Though he didn't blame Jenny, the loss created a huge rift in their relationship. Tensions rose, and not long after, they divorced.

Katie's Story:
Katie's mother died instantly in a motorcycle accident when both she and her partner, who weren't wearing helmets, were thrown from the bike. The death was sudden, unexpected. They had planned to go to a Jimmy Buffett tribute concert together next month. Her grief was overwhelming. She found herself drinking alone every night for months. Her primary relationship fell apart. For a time, grief consumed her. But she eventually rebuilt her life—throwing herself into work, buying a house, cultivating a healthy new relationship, and volunteering to help others in crisis. Her journey was far from easy, but she found a way to promote her healing.

Will's Story:
Will's grief turned into anger and acting out. He got into trouble with family, friends, and at work, eventually landing in jail. Those around him were unsympathetic when he explained that his unresolved grief was driving his behavior. They told him to "get a grip." When grief pours out as anger or tears, it can alienate others. His network flopped and he found himself now dealing with another type of grief – the loss of people he counted on to be his friends.

These stories show how grief can turn people's lives upside down. Perhaps not directly, but certainly indirectly. Grief has its ability to transform our lives into unexpected emotions and paths. The impact of grief should not be underestimated.

Grief can also take us in other directions.

Angie and Andrew's Story
Angie and Andrew had the type of relationship that fairy tales are written about. True love. The perfect relationship. Andrew fell dead with a heart attack. Angie grieved, and shortly afterwards she was found dead at home of a stroke.

Bev's Story
Beverly's goal was to create a childcare center that used love, beauty, creativity, and support so that children and their families could thrive and find delight in every new day. It was her dream come true. Suddenly, funding for her program was ripped away. She was without a job. Her center was forced to close. It was only a few months before she was diagnosed with cancer and died.

William and Martha's Story
William and Martha had spent the bulk of their 70 years together. They both came down with terminal illnesses about the same time. Instead of waiting and watching one another died, they drove their car to a pretty location, covered the seats and inside of the car with plastic. William shot Mary and then himself, leaving a joint goodbye letter inside.

What do these last three stories have in common?
Psychologist James Lynch blames their deaths on an underlying cause he calls "the broken heart."

Managing grief is no small matter!

OK, we understand that grief is normal. But what do we do transform it? There are two major forms.

Introverted and Extroverted Grief: Different Ways of Coping

Introverted grief is when we turn inward to cope with loss.
It's a kind of isolation — a "leave me alone" state — where everyday routines like eating, drinking, bathing, and sleeping fall by the wayside. We may feel deeply depressed, sometimes crying instantly at the smallest memory trigger. Anger, regret, guilt, or a swirl of complex emotions may flood us. We might not want to leave the house, or on the flip side, we might desperately crave noise and distraction to drown out the silence.

Behaviorally, introverted grief can manifest as overindulgence in food or alcohol, binge-watching, or other unusual behaviors. While these responses can be normal for a short time or during occasional low moods, they become unhealthy if they persist. This is often when grief becomes complicated or protracted.

When Maggie's dog died, she didn't want to talk to anyone. She couldn't stand getting text messages that said, "Hugs" from people who didn't understand the intensity of her loss. It took her weeks before she was able to get together with friends again. And even then, she didn't want to talk about it.

Extroverted grief is quite different.

It's about engaging others and sharing our sadness. We look for ways to transform our grief into something positive, to honor and remember the person we lost through social action.

Do you want people to donate money in your memory? Instead of sending flowers, maybe you prefer donations to build a dog park, create a scholarship fund, or support a cause you cared about. There might be memorial events like a "Rachel's Road Race" or a polar plunge fundraiser held in honor of someone special. Communities sometimes name buildings, streets, or airports after beloved individuals. Charities and philanthropies can grow from a person's generosity, inspiring others to give or volunteer.

Survivors and families affected by tragedy sometimes become activists or start movements — like David Hogg who has gotten involved in politics or in the creation of programs like the Sandy Hook Challenge and Choose Love Movement by parents of children lost in Newtown, CT. These acts of remembrance transform grief into purpose, potentially easing the pain by helping others.

People also honor loved ones by lighting candles, visiting graves, organizing fundraisers, wearing memorial T-shirts, placing flowers at places of loss, or creating rituals that feel meaningful. Everyone grieves differently, and we each must find what helps us heal.

Things Not to Say to People Who Are Grieving

- "It's for the best."
- "They're not suffering anymore."
- "They're in heaven."
- "Don't cry."
- "It was meant to be."
- "I understand how you feel."
- "When this happened to me, [insert experience]."
- "They're in a better place."
- "They lived a long life."
- "You'll be OK."

- "How are you doing?"
- "They brought this on themselves."
- "It was inevitable."
- "Get over it."
- "Move on."
- "It was just (a dog, cat, in-law, etc.)."
- "Stay busy."
- "You have to be strong for others."
- "Don't think about it."
- "It was their time."
- "Now you're free."
- "Everything happens for a reason."
- "At least you had them for a while."

The Long Road of Grief

Right after someone dies, there's usually an outpouring of visitors, calls, cards, and casseroles. Then, often, those supports fade away. Many people who are left behind would appreciate an outstretched hand even months or years later, along with invitations to do enjoyable things together.

Other people grieve in ways that may seem, on the surface, that they no longer care about the deceased person.
This is not true.
Moving on doesn't mean forgetting.
Honoring the past while creating a new normal is part of healing.

Different Ways People Grieve

- Barbie's husband had cared for her through a long illness. After she died, he was well supported—but his family expected him to mourn forever. They were surprised and uncomfortable when he started dating soon after. He had grieved for years before Barbie's passing, and her death freed him from caregiving so he could live his own life again. His love for her didn't end; his style of grieving just looked different.

- Frank's wife quickly gave away his clothes and sold the family home less than a week after his death. For friends and family, this felt abrupt and unsettling. But for her, starting fresh helped her cope in her own way.

- Taylor's parents kept their child's room exactly as it was 15 years after Taylor's tragic death. The unmade bed, scattered toys, and unfinished projects keep Taylor present for them and help them to cope with the loss.

Everyone Grieves Differently

There is no right or wrong way to grieve. People may grieve in ways that are unfamiliar or uncomfortable to us—and that's okay. Give space for complicated emotions and tangled relationships to unfold. It took years to create these connections, so it makes sense that unpacking grief will take time, too.

Sometimes grief is deepened by guilt.

Guilt is often the mind's attempt to impose control on a situation that feels utterly out of control. Our brains replay the scenario, trying to "fix" it in hindsight, as if rewriting the past could somehow ease the pain of the present.

We might feel responsible for someone's death—wondering, *Did I do something wrong? Could I have stopped this? Did I miss a chance to help?*

And ultimately – Am I responsible for their dying?

Guilt and regret creep in with all the *"if only"* questions:

- *If only I had called more often.*
- *If only I had gone to visit.*
- *If only we had taken that trip we always talked about.*
- *If only I was a better parent.*
- *If only I was a better child.*
- *The list goes on...*

The "if only" script becomes a loop:

- *If only I had been there...*
- *If only I had said something...*
- *If only I had tried harder...*

We may feel we contributed to the outcome in some way, even when logic tells us otherwise.

Survivor's guilt is also common.

Thoughts like *"It should have been me, not them,"* or *"Why am I still here?"* can haunt us. When someone we love dies unexpectedly or tragically, we may feel like we failed to protect or save them.

These guilty feelings can intensify depression, fuel regret, and increase the risk of prolonged or complicated grief. We may engage in negative self-talk or harsh self-judgment, replaying events and imagining different outcomes over and over.

But let's pause here.

- Could we really have stopped them from dying?
- Were we actually responsible for everything that happened?
- Weren't there likely many other factors at play?

Most of the time, we are not in control of life or death. We are not all-powerful. We don't hold the levers of fate, even if our hearts wish we could.

The past is past.

We can't change it—no matter how much we wish we could.

Releasing the Weight of Guilt

Getting past guilt takes time and conscious effort. But it is possible.

For those of us who are grieving now, we can support one another with loving-kindness and compassion—not criticism or blame.

Let's avoid adding weight to the loads others already carry. Instead, let's help lift the weight when we can.

From a proactive perspective, we can consider how to reduce guilt for those we leave behind.

Creating a Goodbye Plan—one that offers closure, love, forgiveness, and understanding—can help ensure that when our time comes, those we love are not left wondering, blaming, or burdened by regret.

Through Pain there is a Healing Power of Grief

There is a Long Journey when it comes to Grief and Healing.

Grieving is not a straight path. It's a winding, bumpy road that may go on for a long time—possibly forever. But grief will change over time. It won't always feel this raw. When we think of supporting people through their grief, here are some recommendations:

Honor their feelings. People need to talk, and if they trust you enough to share their emotions, allow them to do so without judgment. You don't need to offer advice—especially unsolicited advice! If you don't know what to say, a simple, "I hear you, and I'm sorry," or "Is there anything I can do?" goes a long way.

Listen actively. Mirror back what they say to show you're truly hearing them. Phrases like "This is difficult" or "This is such a tough time" can open the door for deeper conversation.

Be present. Spending time together, regular check-ins by phone or card, and little unexpected gestures—like bringing food or helping with chores—communicate that you care. Showing up to mow the lawn, clean the kitchen, or run errands without being asked can be a welcomed kindness.

Acknowledge the reality. Don't avoid "the elephant in the room." The person died, and there's a lot to process around that truth. Sharing memories can be uplifting, and gently asking about the person who passed away shows interest and respect.

Keep the focus on the grieving person. Don't expect them to manage your feelings or emotional needs. If you need support yourself, find someone else to talk to. It's unkind to turn the conversation toward your own experience when the goal is to help them navigate their grief.

> Yes, the loss may always hurt.
> But, hopefully, one day… it won't hurt *so bad*.
> We can learn to carry it differently.
>
> If grief is a journey,
> it's comforting to have others walk alongside us.
>
> We don't need advice - just someone who listens.
> Together,
> with time and support,
> we'll find our way through it.

IF SADNESS IS GRIEF TURNED INWARDS, ANGER IS GRIEF TURNED OUTWARDS.

Let's now bravely look at how our anger can get in the way of a good goodbye.

ANGER

Anger can be a BIG emotion at the End of Life

Anger often raises its ugly head during times of death.
It can come from the dying person and from those left behind.

Accept this: your passing will send ripples outward into the world—some expected, many unexpected.

Let's look at some real-life stories of death anger. They can help us reflect on our own families, friends, and feelings, and encourage us to make decisions now that might help those we love have better lives and relationships later.

It's All About Me

Anger is a natural - even logical response - when we learn we're dying.
If I realize I'm dying, I might get furious.
And sad. Very sad. Which turns into mad, either directly or indirectly.

We often try to hide this anger by calling it something else—sadness, frustration, fear—but anger is usually at the core.

Here are some common thoughts that reveal what's really going on inside:

- I didn't get to do all the things I wanted to.
- I was just starting to figure things out and now it's over, damn it!
- I'm mad the doctors didn't figure out what was wrong in time.
- Save me! Do something!
- I'm angry at God.
- Why me? Why now?
- I'm sad I never got to visit all those places I dreamed about.
- Life cheated me, and it's not fair.
- I want a second chance—a do-over!

- Why do so many jerks get to live long lives while I, who tried to live well, am dying?
- I'm angry that others don't seem to care about me.
- You said you hated me and wished I was dead—well, now you got your wish.
- It feels like I never really mattered.
- I'm dying but not dead—I'm angry that people keep telling me what to do or making decisions for me.
- Leave me alone.
- Nobody will care when I'm gone.
- I never had the love of my life, and now it's over.
- I spent my life doing for others, and they don't give a damn.
- I'm angry at you, and I don't even know why. You're here, so I'm taking it out on you.
- I should have had more fun and been kinder to myself.
- I was gonna… I was gonna… I was gonna… but now I can't.
- I scrimped and saved for nothing.
- I don't want to die like so-and-so, but I'm scared I might.
- I hate pain and suffering.
- I'm angry that strangers keep doing things to my body like I'm just an object.
- I'm still here—don't talk about me in the past tense.
- It's all too much—I just want to die.
- It all went so fast.
- I'm angry at myself.

Anger is part of life's journey—messy, raw, and real. By naming it, feeling it, and understanding it, we can start to find ways to ease it, for ourselves and for those we leave behind.

People like predictability.
We like to know what is going to happen next.
We tend to be control freaks, truth be known.

Think about the seasons — spring, summer, fall, and winter.
Each one ends, yet new beginnings always follow.

We don't know when our new beginning will be, and that unknown can be scary.
We don't know what is going to happen when we die.
Will it hurt?
Will we fight to hold on to life?
Are there angels?
Will we see our family and friends when we die?
Is there a life review – and will we be humbled by it?
So many questions!

Feeling anger about dying is normal, natural, and inevitable. It's a powerful emotion tied closely to fear. When we feel threatened, frustrated, cheated, or treated unfairly, anger often surfaces.

But what do we do with these powerful, upset emotions? We have to find

Constructive Ways to Deal With Anger

Finding healthy ways to express and manage your anger is important. This might look like:

- Talking with a counselor, clergy member, spiritual companion, good friend, or a death doula
- Joining others who are going through the same experience
- Taking peaceful walks in nature with your dog or by yourself
- Practicing meditation or reading uplifting materials

The first step is acknowledging your anger. If you don't, anger can get misplaced, or displaced, leading to harmful patterns like:

- Taking it out on people trying to help
- Yelling at innocent strangers or loved ones
- Blaming others who have nothing to do with your situation
- Hurting yourself or engaging in risky behaviors like excessive drinking, drug use, reckless driving, or handling weapons irresponsibly
- Exhibiting road rage, breaking things, or hitting objects
- Being physically or verbally abusive
- Screaming at the TV over the news, sports, or others' choices
- Getting annoyed over small things
- Rejecting or alienating those who care about you, then saying, "See, you never really cared anyway."
- Becoming depressed or suicidal
- Engaging in self-sabotage
- Acting out and becoming difficult or hostile

Displaced Anger: A Common Human Experience

Displaced anger happens to everyone at times.

We might yell at the dog, snap at children, or lash out at a clerk, even though they aren't the source of our pain.

Sometimes, we beat ourselves up with blame and shame.

Maybe you've witnessed this in others or even experienced it yourself.

It's easy to forget where the anger truly comes from and to mistakenly target the wrong people or things.

When someone leaves us, the pain isn't just sadness.

There can be anger directed at:

- The person who died
- The illness or accident that caused the death
- The doctor
- Politicians
- Others - the list can be long.

Anger, while painful, is a natural part of the grieving process.

Building a kinder relationship with your anger is a difficult but crucial step.

Remember: One of the biggest relationships you'll have to come to peace with is the one inside yourself.

Anger From Others Who Think It's All About Them

When others learn that you're dying—or after you've passed—they may get angry too.
Your leaving can feel inconvenient for them.
They're sad.
They'll miss you, especially if they've counted on you to always be there.

I've witnessed some royal hissy fits from those left behind. Some people don't just feel upset—they're filled with rage. Others know that outright anger looks bad, so they mask it with passive-aggression. They might smile sweetly but inside they're burning with anger and want to lash out in unacceptable ways.

It's normal for people to be upset, sad, and angry that you're gone.

There are different forms of anger from those left behind.

Other people's anger after a death is transactional—it reflects something they feel or need. Here are three common forms:

- Anger from Missing You
- Anger from Entitlement or Greed
- Anger from Misplaced Frustration or Passive-Aggression

"Missing You" Anger

When someone dies, it disrupts the familiar rhythms of life. We all crave predictability and routine. We assume our partner or spouse will always be there, even if sometimes they get on our nerves. We expect to see family at holidays. Parents build their lives around their children. We have daily habits, like walking the dog before breakfast or sharing evening meals.

When someone we rely on disappears, it throws a wrench into our routine. Suddenly, the person we cooked for isn't there. The listener, the helper—gone. This absence is inconvenient and painful. We must figure out how to fill the gap and adjust our lives. That transition can be rough and unsettling, even if it leads to growth later on.

Common Emotions Tied to Missing You Anger:

- "How dare you leave me!"
- "I need you!"
- "What will I do without you?"
- "Why is life so unfair?"
- "Of all the people who deserved to die, why did God take you?"
- "And why now?"

Anger Stories

Antoinetta's life revolved around Charlie. When he died, she felt lost. She relied on him to pay bills, fix things around the house, drive into the city, and share dinners. They had rituals like watching TV together every night. After he passed, she was angry at him for dying. She threw away the ship-in-the-bottle he had spent weeks building. She stopped going to church, furious at God. Most of all, she was angry because her life had been built around Charlie, and now he was gone. It has been years, and she is still angry at him.

Rafel and his five siblings inherited 26 acres of beautiful countryside and a big family home. Two siblings wanted the house for themselves. Others wanted to sell it and split the proceeds. One sibling claimed she should get the house because she cared for their parents in their final years. Disputes also arose over what to do with the land—sell to developers, keep in trust, donate, or sell to local businesses. Rafel tried to stay positive but the fighting grew so toxic he hasn't spoken to any of his siblings since. His reluctance to fight meant his share was quite small.

Rory was in the ICU recovering from a stroke. One day, four family members of another patient argued loudly in the hall outside over who would get what from their father—who was still alive. The heat of their dispute was intense and heartbreaking. Rory realized that this was a foreshadowing of what was going to happen in her future if she didn't take action soon.

After divorcing Bill, Mary felt hurt and angry when Bill died. His obituary listed his new wife and her children but made no mention of Mary, despite her having been a major part of his life. She felt entitled to be recognized in his passing. While divorced, his passing triggered grieving the loss of a shared past.

Entitlement Anger

This type of anger is very common—perhaps the most common form of anger after a death. It arises when people feel they haven't been treated as specially or as fairly as they believe they deserve. We might feel the deceased owed us something, or that they had something we want or think rightfully belongs to us. At funerals, anger can flare when our relationship with the deceased isn't recognized as a priority. We feel left out or overlooked, convinced we deserve more.

Common Objects of Entitlement Anger

- Money: cash, stocks, bonds
- Property: houses, land, cars, boats
- Business assets: ownership shares, licenses, brands
- Sentimental objects: photos, books, tools, kitchenware
- Valuable items: jewelry, artwork, musical instruments, antiques, silverware

Sometimes these things are carefully assigned in a will. But many items might not be listed, leading to fights. If there's no will, family disputes over inheritance can explode. Even with a will, conflicts may arise because someone feels left out or cheated.

Anger can be extensive and extreme when people fight over things that have a lot of monetary value. Seth fought for his mom's Stradivarius violin; Arnie fought for ownership of his family's grocery store chain; Sam fought for rights to his dad's music; Marnie fought for her grandmother's jewelry.

Another problem is secrecy—sometimes the person handling the estate doesn't fully disclose what's there or what the will says. This can breed resentment and deceit. For instance, a Maggie observed, "I was never given a copy of the will for anyone in my family who passed away. Maybe I was left something, or maybe not. By not sharing a copy, it logically engenders suspicion."

Voices of Entitlement Anger: You might hear things like:

- "Mama always said I could have that."
- "That was supposed to be mine."
- "You don't deserve that."
- "You're taking more than your fair share."
- "You're not dividing things equally."
- "I built the business; you don't deserve any of it."
- "You don't need it but I do."
- "You never really cared about it (or them)."

This type of anger can be found in any family, whether rich or poor. The news is regularly filled with articles about family feuds over who gets what when somebody dies.

Famous Family Wars Over Inheritance include:

- Michael Jackson's will was contested as possibly fake.
- Jimi Hendrix died intestate, causing fights over his estate.
- Nelson Mandela's house was left out of his will, leading to disputes.
- Martin Luther King Jr.'s children have fought over alleged misappropriation of his estate.
- Leona Helmsley left $12 million to her dog but nothing to some grandchildren.

- J. Howard Marshall's estate was contested by Anna Nicole Smith against his son.

Famous families may fight over bigger assets, but the dynamics are essentially the same that most families face.

We, like these famous families, could create clear, thoughtful GoodBye plans so many legal battles could be avoided.

Misplaced Anger

It's not unusual to see people act in ways that seem illogical or even irrational when coping with death. People are not fighting over things of financial value. They are fighting over more elusive, symbolic, relational issues. They may be fighting over an object or how a memorial service is being conducted, but this happens because the visible argument or conflict isn't really the true underlying cause of their feelings. There are underlying issues that have likely been seething and growing for quite some time before.

Why Do Families Fight Over Meaningless Things?
Families sometimes battle over photos of ancestors they never met or items with no monetary or aesthetic value—simply because those things were important to someone else.

The Story of Clare and Sarah:

Clare and Sarah grew up hearing their father's war stories. He had a treasured piece of metal he brought back from battle—a symbol that meant a lot to him. When he passed away, both sisters wanted to keep it. Clare, who lived with their father, declared, "It's MINE." Sarah shot back, "It's just as much mine as yours." They fought over that one-inch piece of metal for decades. After they passed, their daughters continued the feud—fighting over an object connected to a man none of them ever knew.

What made that little piece of metal so valuable? Because it was important to their father, and they loved him, their minds tricked them into caring deeply about the object itself—even if, in reality, it held no real meaning or practical use to them.

Items of sentimental value can trigger extreme upset or anger. When Karen's mom died, all she wanted was her mom's wooden spoon since it reminded her of all the dishes they had cooked together as she grew up. Her brother gave all her dishes and kitchen items to charity without asking her if she wanted anything.

We hold onto possessions because they trigger memories we want to keep alive. For example, I keep certain kitchen items my mom used because when I use them, I feel close to her. But did she truly cherish those pots and dishes? Probably not—they were just convenient at the time. We may attribute more meaning to objects than the owners ever intended or felt.

When I was a child I bought a special Hummel figurine while on a family trip to Germany. I carried it on the plane so it wouldn't get broken. I put it in a place of honor in our home. While I was away at college, my mom gave it away to someone else. It was mine. I felt hurt, cheated. And I was angry.

But why? It was a just material object. That is all. I could buy another. Mama is long dead. She thought she was doing something thoughtful for someone – it never occurred to her that she was being thoughtless to me. So it usually isn't the objects that hurt us as much as the symbolic meaning behind them.

Sometimes, we cling to things—and anger—for reasons that, when we step back, seem quite irrational.

Intergenerational Anger often passes down through generations. When someone feels wronged or denied what they deserved, that grievance can be handed down as a family legacy.

Cliques may form, and sides may be taken, breeding distrust and animosity between branches of the same family.

Harold and his brothers were treated unequally by their parents. One became a banker, one a plumber, one a truck driver. Their vastly different lives created divides—while the truck driver's children struggle financially, the banker's descendants don't understand why. Two generations later, these cousins rarely see or speak to each other, torn apart largely by a decision made by their great-grandparents over property inheritance.

Carrying Other People's Anger is Dysfunctional, you know.

It's easy to inherit someone else's resentment. We might dislike someone simply because a family member did, even without knowing them or having any personal experience with them. Death, funerals, and inheritance disputes often stir up old, unresolved tensions that spill over in unexpected ways.

The Case of JR:
JR was a divisive community figure—loved by some, hated by others. Known for his sharp tongue, wit, and blunt style, he often alienated people. He talked trash about even people in his family. After his death, his wife and children chose to exclude his only brother from any funeral events or gatherings. The brother sat alone, wondering what JR had said about him to cause such coldness. Why, in a moment that called for healing, was anger allowed to rule?

Amanda's Story:
Amanda dislikes her husband's extended family. Though her husband left financial gifts in his will for his nieces and nephews, Amanda has chosen to keep this secret. The children don't know about the inheritance, and she isn't telling them—legally, she doesn't have to. Why deny the kids their uncle's gift? Because Amanda clings to an old grudge against their mother, perpetuating conflict long after the root cause has faded.

How a GoodBye Plan Can Help

We can remember, honor, and love—without drowning in guilt, grief, or anger.

When we honestly review our lives, we see our successes, our failures, our secret selves, and our regrets.

Our lives have been roller coasters, with ups and downs, ins and outs.

All of them have added threads to the tapestry of our life.

Our life review is for us.

Our lives, after all, belong to no one but us.

There may be parts that we want to share and that others would like to know.

Or not.

What we do with our stories and secrets can bring either comfort or distress. And we must remember: death, like life, is transactional. Like ripples on water, our lives merge into one another.

Take time to think about what you want to do.

While all sorts of emotions rise up when we contemplate leaving, anger is a particularly tricky emotion. It often hides behind other feelings and disguises itself to seem less harmful than it is. It seeks to rally others to its cause, creating "sides" and deepening divisions.

While anger is a natural human response, it stands in the way of healing and moving forward. It rarely contributes to a peaceful, respectful GoodBye.

While planning who gets what may feel like a chore, creating a GoodBye plan is a gift to those you leave behind. You can use a will, or even a notarized letter, to clearly state your wishes.

Think about Nancy and Chase's Family Meeting

Though not planning to die soon, Nancy and Chase called all their children together. They shared with them exactly how they wanted their assets divided—and why. They went through each room, each item, and discussed who would receive what.

This transparency helped prevent confusion and conflict. More importantly, it taught their children respect, generosity, and negotiation skills. Their grandchildren watched and learned about compassionate relationships and how to work through difficult conversations with love.

When developing your exit plan, it's wise to anticipate the potholes others might fall into. Consider how to encourage kindness and reduce conflict.

We've spent our lives loving people—think about the conversations you can have now and the strategies you can set in motion to help your family move forward smoothly and lovingly when you're gone.

Creating small rituals, gentle conversations, and meaningful Goodbyes can ease the burden for those who come after us.

This is the focus of the next chapter.

7

The Importance of Ceremonies

The Importance of Ceremonies

Do you want a GoodBye party?

You could have one before you pass away.
After you're gone.
Or not at all.

Whether you want one is worth considering.
Because both life and death are relational.

Focus…

Do we need a prize or public performance to prove that we mattered?
No - but perhaps it is something worth considering.
Maybe for us.
And maybe for those we are leaving behind
Who have shaped our life so profoundly.

When someone we love dies, it hurts.
Really hurts.

There's a raw pain that eats away at the core of us.
We wonder how we'll go on without them.
And just as we'll leave a gap in others' lives when we die, their absence leaves a hole in ours.

People will have to adjust.
But how they do that is personal.

There's no formula for how to grieve, how long to mourn, or what it should look like.

Grief, like love, is as unique as the people who experience it.

We exist because of love.
We keep going because of the connections we have—with people, places, ideas, passions, dreams.
Relationships give life meaning.
And our dying—just like our living—is deeply relational.

So do you want a GoodBye party for you – or for them?
And if you do, what do you want it to look like?

That's the focus of this chapter.

Saying Goodbye, Your Way

When we die, perhaps it is appropriate to have a *going-away party*.

Not to mourn the end, but to honor the journey.

When someone sets off on a grand adventure, we often feel both joy and sorrow:

- Joy for what we shared
- Joy for what lies ahead.
- Sorrow because we will miss them.
- Sorrow because we can't go with them—yet.

Grief reminds us of love.
And death reminds us that *love never truly ends.*

In life and in death We Are All In This Together

As this book has said time and again:

Death is transactional.
It is relational.
Our death is ours—but it will also impact those we love.
Their death is theirs—but it will shape us forever.
So, each life—and each death—is a shared story we must all work out in our own way.

Together.
With honesty.
With grace.
And with love.

Funerals, Relationships, and the Relational Journey of Death

A funeral is the most common celebration of life that the majority of people may experience.

form of a funeral can vary from extreme sadness to unparalleled gratitude and joy.

Funerals are less about the person who has died and more for those left behind.

The one who has passed on has already moved into whatever comes next.

For the rest of us—those who stay—funerals can offer a way to reflect on the past, understand what happened, and consider how to move forward.

There is no requirement—legal or moral—that anyone must have a funeral or memorial service.

Around the world, many people pass without any formal ceremony to commemorate their life.

In some cultures, birth and death are seen as natural transitions—no grand ritual required.

If family and friends want to gather, to bond, share memories, and grieve together, they are welcome to do so. But ultimately, grief is deeply personal.

For some, public grieving rituals help. For others, they can feel like added pain or pressure.

Rethinking Funerals

Historically, funerals were held to honor a person's contributions and offer closure. Thoughtful, heartfelt, meaningful.

But in today's world, funerals can become highly orchestrated productions—much like weddings—requiring months of planning and thousands of dollars.

The funeral industry, like the wedding industry, has built a lucrative economy around grief.

We're taught that grief at a funeral should look a certain way: black clothes, tears, silence, solemnity.

But around the world, a counter-movement is growing.

In some cultures, death is a celebration—of a life well lived, of a spirit moving on, of love that transcends.
The Death Positive Movement is promoting a counter to the sad and bad model of death.
But positivity focused funerals and more joyous and thoughtful death ceremonies are nothing new.

The shifting of the death narrative is part of a broader cultural shift.
Grief is personal.
So is remembrance.

Some people need a crowd to feel comforted; others prefer quiet solitude.

Here are true stories that show the many ways we honor those we love, mourn those we've lost, and begin the long walk forward without them.

Celebrations of Life: Real Stories of Grief, Goodbye, and Grace

Anna's Wish

Anna lived in a modest home just down the street from the cemetery. From her front porch, she watched the funeral processions roll by—some with long trails of cars, others with just a few. She'd shake her head and say, "I don't want no skimpy funeral," as if her children could control how many would come. When Anna passed away at 103, her children held their breath, unsure of what to expect. To their relief, many people showed up. Anna got what she wanted: not a skimpy funeral, but a full celebration of her long, observant life.

Mary's Masterpiece

Mary had terminal cancer, and there was no saving her. But she took control of her farewell. She selected her favorite dinnerware, coordinated the catering menu, picked out the flowers and where they'd be placed in the house. She chose the music and prepared thank-you notes and a handout of memories and wishes she wanted people to carry forward. Mary didn't wait for someone else to organize her goodbye. She bravely designed a parting gift to those she loved—one last gathering where her presence was felt in every detail.

Mr. and Mrs. W.: No Funeral, Just Flowers

The W. family believed that funerals were not necessary. There was no law requiring one, and they saw no need for a formal service or expense. They were cremated and asked for their ashes to be scattered in the garden at a relative's home. When both had passed, their ashes were combined in that peaceful garden. That spring, a pair of turtle doves built a nest in the tree above. The family saw this not as coincidence, but as connection—an eternal love story continuing among the blossoms.

Mrs. LePage Dances Again

Mrs. LePage lived nearly a century. Her life wasn't easy, especially after she lost both legs and spent her final decades in a wheelchair. But she was fiercely independent, loved birds and music, and was deeply cherished by her family and community. Her funeral was joyful and unforgettable. A packed church heard stories of her grit, humor, and love. A Dixieland band played her favorite songs. At the end, the band marched down the aisle playing *"When the Saints Go Marching In."* The family followed in a kind of second line parade, followed by everyone else who met in the lobby where people danced. They celebrated. And in their dancing, it felt like Mrs. LePage—free from her wheelchair at last—was dancing with them.

Little Aiden's Last Flight

Aiden was only two when he passed away from a rare condition that slowly turned his muscles to stone. His parents gave him the most joyful, love-filled life they could. He went to daycare. He played. He made friends. When he died, his family carried his tiny, hand-decorated coffin to the cemetery. They placed him gently into the earth and sang to him. Then they released dozens of origami doves into the sky. While his time was short, his impact was enormous. The community gathered in shared grief, offering the kind of support that helped his family begin to heal.

Morrie's Unfinished Goodbye

Morrie died young, shortly after receiving a corrected medical diagnosis that came too late. He had a will—but no plan for how he wanted to be remembered. His sister, the legal executor, organized a funeral that aligned with her wishes - not his. Morrie's children, knowing what he would have wanted, were powerless to change the arrangements. Feeling cheated without the chance to gather with others who loved him, their grief felt heavy and lonely—made worse by the conflict surrounding his death. Alone and lonely, they created a private ceremony to bury his ashes in a place he loved.

Richie's Spectacle

Richie was a well-known politician and businessman. When he died, his funeral was less a goodbye and more a public spectacle. People came not just to mourn, but to be seen. Local politicians used the wake as a campaign stop. Richie's old girlfriends offered syrupy condolences to his stunned widow. Photographers captured the tears of his children in uninvited, invasive snapshots. Everyone was there—but the real question hung in the air: *Who was this funeral actually for?*

What These Stories Teach Us

These true stories remind us that:

- Some people want a full house. Others want only the wind and the trees.
- Some plan every last detail. Others leave no map behind.
- Some ceremonies lift us up. Others leave us empty.

There is no one right way to say goodbye.

Goodbye Ceremonies: Do It Your Way

Goodbye ceremonies can be deeply meaningful for individuals and communities.

But they are not a requirement.

Making a public event out of someone's passing is sometimes comforting, and other times it may feel unnecessary—or even harmful.

Grief is personal. Mourning doesn't come in a one-size-fits-all format.

Different cultures, religions, and families shape the way we think grief *should* look.

Sine traditions expect quiet sorrow, others welcome loud public expressions.

Some people need a large, organized goodbye; others prefer to process grief privately or not at all.

Some move through grief quickly. For others, it may take years.

The bottom line: You don't have to do it their way.

If a traditional way brings you comfort—wonderful. Follow it.
But if it doesn't feel right, then it's okay to do it your own way.
Listening to your own voice is key.
hat is how you write the final chapter of your own story.

How to Plan *Your* Goodbye Celebration

In order to leave everything neatly tied up, it's important to be attentive to detail.

Think of a celebration like creating a party, a wedding, the office annual meeting.

There are three stages to making a successful celebration.

First, there is the preparation of everything that needs to be done for the big event.

Then there is the big event.

This is followed by cleaning up from the event.

If you plan for it now, you give your loved ones the clarity, comfort, and peace of knowing they're doing exactly what *you* wanted.

This means if you want to create a good GoodBye, there are things you have to do ahead of time in order to make it a smooth, positive, successful occurrence.

Step 1: Ask yourself: Who are you?
How do you want to be remembered? What legacy do you want to leave? Your answer guides everything else.

Step 2: What do you want others to know?
What stories from your life do you want people to carry forward?
What would your "goodbye message" be? You're in charge of it, you know.

Step 3: Make a Will and Create Documents
A will is a legal document that explains how your assets should be distributed and who will carry out your wishes.
Without one, decisions are left up to the courts—and family fights are more likely.

Here are guidelines to help you.

How to Make a Will

- Hire a lawyer.
- Use an online service.
- Or write your wishes and have them notarized.

Just get something in writing. It's one of the kindest things you can do for the people you leave behind.

There are many different types of Wills. Here's a quick guide to what kind of will you might want:

1. Living Will
   Explains your wishes for medical care if you can't speak for yourself.
   (Life support? Organ donation?)
2. Formal or Standard Will
   A typed document signed by witnesses—legally solid and traditional.
3. Simple Will
   Basic instructions on who inherits what and who your executor is.
4. Joint Will
   Used by couples who want the same outcomes after both pass.
5. Testamentary Trust Will
   Creates a trust for children or others with detailed instructions on how assets are handled.
6. Holographic Will
   A handwritten will without witnesses. It may be challenged in court, depending on your state laws.

Your will can be as elaborate and detailed as you want. You can hire an attorney and make it very formal. Or you can write up what you want and get it signed by a notary public at no cost. Creating a will doesn't have to be complicated or expensive. Having something is better than nothing. Your loved ones will need to have your guidance in order to avoid conflict.

If you share what you need and want—while you can—it's a gift to those around you.

Take Robbie, for example. When he died, there was no paper trail. No:

- Record of credit cards or bank accounts
- List of passwords for websites
- Info about life insurance—or whether it even existed
- Name of the mortgage company or account number
- Utility providers or contact info
- Clarity on who the current lawyer or accountant was

An outdated, handwritten will was eventually found in the china cabinet—but was it even valid?

Robbie's family was left scrambling. They had to dig through drawers, files, old bills, voicemails, and desk piles—trying to piece together his life, while grieving his death. It was stressful, exhausting, and could have been avoided.

Ask Yourself:
Do you have a list of these things somewhere?

- Banks, credit cards, and account numbers
- Insurance policies
- Mortgage and home documents
- Utility accounts
- Lawyer, accountant, and executor contacts
- Passwords for essential websites
- Burial or memorial wishes
- A current, accessible will

Most of us intend to get it together. We think we have time.

But the truth is—we don't know when that time will run out.

A sudden health episode.
A car accident.
A fall.
A diagnosis we didn't see coming.
Life can change on a dime.
Having everything in one central place helps not only those you leave behind—it helps you while you're still here.

And let's face it: most of us don't have pristine filing systems.
Scattered sticky notes, inbox folders, glove compartments, and "safe places" we'll never remember… that won't help anyone.

Pick a method and stick with it. A binder. A file. A shared folder. A password manager. Just make sure someone trustworthy knows where it is.

Choose Your Executor Carefully

The executor is the person responsible for carrying out your will. They will:

- Pay your bills,
- Manage your assets,
- Distribute what you leave behind.

Pick someone who is trustworthy, fair, kind, and competent—not just convenient.

Also choose a backup.

Ask yourself:

Who would I *not* want in charge?
Who might stir up drama or mishandle things?

Name the person you trust to do right by you and those you care about.

Make Arrangements for Dependents

People and pets may be counting on your long term care.
Don't let them down!
a plan for how to care for them, financially but also physically.

This includes:

- Children
- Elderly relatives
- Pets
- Anyone who relies on your care

Make sure their needs are clearly addressed in your will.

Be Clear About Who Gets What

If you don't spell it out, your executor will have to make the decisions. That opens the door to hurt feelings, legal challenges, or unfairness.

Step 4 – Make Decisions About Your Body: It's Your Choice

Let's get real: this is your body.
happens to it after you die should be your decision—not anyone else's.

Don't focus on what others want.
Think about what *you* want.

Do you want a Burial, Cremation, or Other Option?
These are the most common choices:

- Natural Burial – no embalming, simple biodegradable casket, often in a green cemetery.
- Embalmed Burial – traditional, with a casket and plot in a cemetery.
- Cremation – ashes can be stored, buried, or scattered.

Sure, there are fancier options for the wealthy, but for most people, it comes down to these three. Choose what fits you best.

What Happens to Your Remains?

- Do you want to be buried in a specific cemetery? If so, leave paperwork or buy the plot in advance.
- Have you inherited or already purchased a burial spot? Document it clearly.
- If cremated, where should your ashes go? Be specific—don't leave your loved ones guessing.
- Consider the container: What kind of coffin, casket, or urn do you want? You can even pick it out yourself to avoid confusion or arguments later.
- If you are doing a burial at sea, where is the area that you desire to rest?

If all this feels too overwhelming now, at least leave *some guidance*. A few notes can spare your loved ones stress and second-guessing.

Step 5 – Decide Who Gets What (The Personal Stuff)

A will handles the big financial stuff—but what about the rest of your "stuff"?

The things that fill your home and life?

Some items may seem ordinary, but they hold emotional weight. Others are valuable or complicated to divide.

Avoid family drama by being clear.

You can:

- Write a list
- Make a video
- Host a (careful!) family meeting
  (Just know: family meetings can bring up tensions, especially around inheritances.)

Consider These Items:

A. Businesses or Ownerships – If you have any business ties or investments, decide exactly who gets what. Be legal and specific.

B. Your Home and Real Estate – Who inherits it, or should it be sold?

C. Vehicles – Cars, boats, motorcycles—make it clear who gets what.

D. Valuables – Jewelry, art, tools, instruments, books. These can become battlegrounds unless clearly assigned.

E. Furniture – Some may be valuable, but more often it holds sentimental value. Say who gets what if it matters to you.

F. Electronics – Especially your computer or phone. Leave passwords in a secure, accessible way. Decide who can access your digital files.

G. Pets – They're family. Decide who will care for them. Arrange backup plans and leave money for their care if needed.

H. Sentimental Objects – Items with little monetary value but huge emotional meaning. Say who should have them. Write a note explaining why, if you'd like.

Vagueness causes confusion. Be specific. If you don't, they won't know what you want.

Step 6 – Decide If You Want a Goodbye Event

You don't *have* to have a funeral, memorial, or celebration.

But if you do want something, you get to decide exactly what it looks like.

Make it solemn or silly. Traditional or totally out-of-the-box.

Make it yours.

Where Should It Happen?

Church? Funeral home? Graveside? Backyard? Beach? Mountaintop? You choose.

When Should It Happen?

- Right after your death?
- A week later to allow people time to travel?
- A month later? A year later?

Pick what feels right to you.

Who Should Lead It?

Someone needs to be the point person to make it happen—like a master of ceremonies.

Options include:

- Clergy
- Family member
- Friend
- Colleague
- Choose someone you trust to represent your wishes and voice.

Who Do You Want to Be There?

Make a list of important people—family, friends, work colleagues, teammates.

contact info so your loved ones can invite them. Kind of think of it as a party invitation.

Pick people you like, that you've cared about, and think that maybe they cared about you.'

Who Should NOT Be There?

It's your goodbye.

If someone has made you feel unsafe or unwelcome in life, you don't have to include them in your death.

are some people we just don't like, who haven't been nice to us, and we don't want to be around them in life or in death.

Say it now so your boundaries are honored later.

Who cares if they get mad?

be gone anyway, and finally have your say.

What Should Happen at the Event?

You can be creative here. Ideas include:

- Specific songs, readings, prayers, or film clips
- Opportunity for people to speak about you—or not
- A party or activity: Potluck, poetry night, softball game, hike, campfire stories, music jam, karaoke, beach picnic
- Memorial rituals: Passing the peace, lighting candles, folding origami, planting trees

This is your final party—make it reflect who you are.
Want dancing? Have dancing.
Want it quiet and reflective? Make it so.
No rules. Just what You want for Your send-off.

Still Not Sure You Want a Goodbye Event?

That's okay too.
You can choose a big, grand affair—or none at all.
Your farewell can be whispered in prayer, a quiet scattering of ashes, or a grand sendoff with fireworks and fanfare.

It's up to you. DO IT YOUR WAY

Step 7 – Tie Up Loose Ends

Everybody has them. What are yours?

Maybe there are legal or financial matters you haven't handled yet.
left undone, they could become a burden to others.
them up now—it's one of the kindest things you can do.
But beyond logistics, let's talk about your heart.

- Is there someone you've loved and never told?

- Is there someone who hurt you, and you want them to know how you feel?
- Are there words you've been meaning to say but haven't had the courage to?

This is your moment.

Act as if there is no tomorrow.

Write a letter.
Make a video.
Record a message.
Tell your stories.
Speak your truth.

These words and memories will become treasures for those you leave behind.

A voice message or handwritten note saying, *"I love you. You mattered to me. Thank you."* can help someone you love heal, grow, and smile again after you're gone.

You don't need to be famous to leave a legacy.
Your words are your legacy.
Use them.

Step 8 – Make Sure Someone Knows Where Everything Is

If you've gone to the effort to make a GoodBye Plan—don't hide it! Let someone you trust know:

- Where your important documents are
- What your wishes are

- How to access things like your will, passwords, accounts, or instructions

You don't need a fancy folder or binder. A clear note, a shared file, or a simple conversation can do wonders.

Give your people the gift of knowing what to do and how to honor you. It saves stress. It avoids confusion. It lets your love shine through.

A Word to the Wise: Celebrate While You're Alive

Don't wait for a funeral to have a celebration.

Throw your own party while you're still here to enjoy it.

- A backyard barbecue
- A dinner with friends
- A beach day
- A picnic "just because it's Thursday"

It doesn't have to be called a "goodbye party."

Make it a holiday party, a birthday party, a movie marathon night—whatever makes you happy.

The people who love you will be glad just to be with you.

Want to be poetic about it? Say you're going on a trip.

You wouldn't be lying—you're just not saying *where* you're going.

Final Reminders

Celebrate LIFE.
Celebrate LOVE.

Celebrate OTHERS.
Celebrate YOU.

And most importantly—don't wait.

8

Death as a Business Transaction

GoodBye decisions you need to consider

Life is sacred. Every day is a gift, a blessing, a miracle waiting to unfold.

Death, in turn, is not the end—it's a spiritual transformation.
A crossing over.
A journey into the unknown.
It is one of the most profound events we will ever experience.

Death, like life, is deeply relational.
face it not only as individuals, but also in relationship—with ourselves, with others, and with the Divine, however we define that.

But here's a truth we don't like to think about:

- Someone is going to have to deal with your body after you die.
- You won't look like yourself.
- You won't move, breathe, or speak.
- Your body will need to be moved—from the place you die to the place you rest.

- That will be physically and emotionally challenging for someone.
- And—make no mistake—**it will be expensive.**

Your Body as a Commodity

Another uncomfortable reality?
Your death is a business opportunity for lots of people.

Funeral homes, crematoriums, florists, cemeteries, obituary writers, transport services—they all make money from your passing. Many of these professionals are kind, compassionate, and helpful. But behind the sympathy cards and soothing voices, it's still a for-profit industry.

They're selling:

- Services
- Support
- Products
- Packages
- "Necessary" add-ons

...all while your loved ones are vulnerable, grieving, and unsure what's required.

Ouch.

Some of these costs are necessary.
Others are optional. Some are pure marketing.
And if *you* don't make your wishes clear, someone else will have to make emotional (and financial) decisions in a moment of distress.

What Actually Happens?

When you die, a whole series of transactions begins. These include decisions around:

- Who handles your body immediately after death
  (Hospital? Home care? Medical examiner? Mortician?)
- Where your body or ashes will go
  (Cemetery? Cremation garden? Scattered in a meaningful place?)
- Whether you want a funeral, memorial, or no service at all
  (Traditional, spiritual, secular, creative, private?)
- Who organizes and officiates the service
  (Clergy? Celebrant? Family or friends?)
- What happens at the service
  (Music, rituals, readings, eulogies, dancing, quiet prayer?)
- Gifts or remembrances for mourners
  (Photos, quote cards, candles, keepsakes?)

And that's just the human and emotional side.

On the legal side, attorneys and estate planners handle the transfer of your assets and belongings.

the physical side, morticians focus on "your remains"—the body that once bloomed with life and love.

Peeling Back the Curtain

The late author Jessica Mitford was one of the first to peel back the curtain in her eye-opening book *The American Way of Death*. She exposed the funeral industry's tendency to upsell grieving families during their most fragile moments—offering caskets with "gasketed sealing systems," high-priced embalming, or pricey packages that imply love equals money.

It's worth remembering:

You do not have to buy what you don't want.
You get to decide how simple or elaborate your death will be.

Goodbye Decisions You Need to Know About

The Funeral (or Death) Industrial Complex

When we think about death, we might picture a funeral home, a casket, some flowers, and a service. It seems simple. Naively, many people believe they're just dealing with a funeral director. But what they don't realize is this:

The mortician is just the gatekeeper to a sprawling, profit-driven industry.

This larger system—the funeral industrial complex—includes a wide array of people, products, and services built around profiting from death. And like any well-oiled machine, it has sales tactics, emotional leverage points, and hidden costs.

Some services are valuable. Many professionals are sincere and compassionate.

But at its core, this is a business. And the customer—grieving, vulnerable, and often overwhelmed—is a sitting duck.

As Maggot Gray explores in *Rot and Roll: Natural Burial and the Funeral Industrial Complex* and Caitlin Doughty beautifully documents in *From Here to Eternity: Traveling the World to Find the Good Death*, there are other ways to approach death.

But first, we need to understand the system we're walking into.

Profiting from Pain

The funeral industry isn't just about handling remains—it's about selling comfort, status, and symbols to those left behind.

Here are just a few of the transactional elements you or your family may face:

- **Body transport and storage**
- **Preparation: embalming, makeup, clothing**
- **Viewing or wake setup**
- **Casket and burial plot selection**
- **Floral arrangements, video slideshows, memory tables**
- **Funeral service planning and hosting**
- **Keepsakes and "mourner gifts"**
- **Catering, music, programs, and more**

Some of these are meaningful and intentional. Others are about up-selling grief—convincing people that love is measured in dollars.

You don't have to fall into that trap.

As the old Holiday Inn motto says:
"The best surprise is no surprise."

By learning the ins and outs of death care, you can plan your GoodBye on *your* terms—and avoid decisions made from pressure, guilt, or confusion.

Transactional Caregiving: Love, Obligation, and Exploitation

Death doesn't start the day we die. It often begins during a long period of decline, when caregiving becomes necessary. And here, too, is an uncomfortable truth:

Caregiving is often transactional. Sometimes care is given freely—out of love, loyalty, or duty. But other times:

- It's given with strings attached.
- It comes with emotional manipulation.
- It's delivered in exchange for money, gifts, or inheritance.
- It becomes a subtle—or not-so-subtle—form of exploitation.

Hard Stories, Hard Lessons

Let's take a closer look at some real-life situations that reflect how transactional caregiving can become harmful.

Grandma and the Car
After Grandma lost her driver's license (she'd accidentally hit a child near a school), she refused to give up her car. Her caregiver, Martha, was hired by Grandma's children and paid to cook, clean, and help out. One day, Martha started using the car to drive Grandma on errands. Then she asked to use it on her own. Eventually, she convinced Grandma to sign the title over to her—after all, she was "doing all the care." Grandma, isolated and manipulated to believe her kids

didn't care, gave away something valuable that she still considered her own.

Aunt Edie's Missing Memories

Placed in a nursing home after she could no longer care for herself, Aunt Edie brought her most precious possessions: her handmade quilt, her rosary, and a necklace with a cross. Over time, each of these items mysteriously disappeared. "Lost in the laundry." "Accidentally thrown away." Staff turnover was high; pay was low. She couldn't prove they were stolen. It was easy for the staff to say she had misplaced them. With no consistent oversight, these small acts of theft added insult to an already difficult life transition.

Mama and the Cake Stand

Mama had a cake stand shaped like a giant strawberry shortcake. Her caregiver admired it and asked for it outright. Mama hesitated. She liked that plate but she was worried the caregiver might stop coming if she refused—so she handed it over. Later, the caregiver asked if her disabled son could stay at the house while she worked. Mama, uncomfortable but afraid to say no, agreed. Partially paralyzed from a stroke, she felt vulnerable and knew she needed help. The caregiver's son was disruptive, and money began disappearing from Mama's purse. Of course, she could not prove it.

Each of these stories show how vulnerability and dependence can be exploited—even by people hired under the banner of compassionate care.

The Caregiving Industry: A Subsystem of the Death Industry

In all three cases above, the caregivers were part of organizations:

- One was run by a religious nonprofit.

- Another by a for-profit nursing facility.
- All were trusted—and that trust was taken advantage of.

The caregiving industry, like the funeral industry, has expanded into a multi-billion-dollar sector. There are agencies, businesses, and institutions that serve the dying and elderly. Some do so with ethics and compassion. Others cut corners, look the other way, or simply don't vet their workers well.

Care, in our system, is often for sale.

And not all caregivers are saints.

Caveat Emptor: Let the Buyer Beware

If you or your loved ones are hiring caregivers, make sure to:

- Check backgrounds and references
- Review contracts carefully
- Monitor valuables and documents
- Stay connected and informed
- Empower the person receiving care to speak up

Whether it's caregiving or funeral planning, it's your job to be informed. Knowledge gives you control. And control is the antidote to exploitation.

Picking Up Your Body: Where You Die and What Happens Next

Chances are, you're not going to die at the funeral home.

Your final moment might happen at home, in a hospital, in a car, in a store, on a trail, in a pool, or anywhere else life takes you. But once someone realizes your soul has left your body, there's a universal next step: getting your body picked up and transported to a place where trained professionals know what to do with it.

That "container" you've lived in—your physical body—could still look serene, like you're sleeping. Or, depending on the circumstances, your body might have been through trauma and no longer resembles your usual self.

Either way, your body will need to be handled, and quickly. That's where death care professionals come in.

Why Moving a Dead Body is Hard

People are often surprised at how heavy a body feels after death. That's not because we gain weight, but because our muscles no longer support us. When we're alive, we use our strength and posture to hold ourselves together—our arms, legs, and core keep everything in place.

But when we die:

- Muscles go limp, and we become what's commonly called "dead weight."
- Our limbs may flop outward, making lifting or repositioning awkward and difficult.
- Soon after death, rigor mortis sets in—muscles stiffen, first in the face and jaw, then throughout the body.
- This stiffness makes the body unyielding, requiring more effort (and more people) to move or transport it safely.

That's why licensed professionals use stretchers, body bags, and teams to carefully and respectfully transport the deceased. It's not a job for the unprepared—it's a physically and emotionally complex task, and it's best left to those trained to do it well.

Where Do You Want Your Body to Go?

Know Your Options Before Others Decide for You.

Once your body is picked up, the next question is: what happens to it?

You have options. Some of the most common include:

- Embalming and Burial
- Cremation
- Natural or Green Burial

And after that, you or your loved ones will choose:

- Where your remains will go (cemetery, ocean, memorial garden, urn, or other final resting places)
- How you will be remembered (funeral, celebration of life, ritual, etc.)

We'll go over all of these in detail so you can choose what feels right for you—not just what's expected or convenient.

The Way Things Have Always Been Done Might Not Be What You Want

In the Midwest town where I grew up, there was a clear formula for what happened when someone died:

1. The body was embalmed and dressed in their Sunday best.
2. There were visiting hours at the funeral home for 1–2 days.
3. A funeral service followed, led by clergy at the funeral home or church.
4. The family processed by car to the cemetery for a graveside service.
5. Friends and family gathered afterward for food and shared stories.
6. Cemetery staff buried the body after the mourners left.

That's the script my parents, grandparents, brother, and extended family followed. There was even a sense of brand loyalty—we always used the same funeral director: Tuck Coots. (That's not his real name—it's his nickname, because he "tucks" people into the ground.)

There's comfort in tradition. But that's not the type of GoodBye I want.

If I don't speak up and make my wishes clear, though, that's probably what I'll get.

Not because my family is trying to override me, but because people default to what they know.

Culture, Religion, and Assumptions About Death

Your family, your community, or your religion may have long-standing traditions about what should happen to your body after death. Religion and culture give us some standard about what "should" happen:

- Jewish, with customs around washing, wrapping, and burial within 24 hours;
- Muslim, with prayer rituals and swift burial facing Mecca;
- Catholic, with a funeral Mass and sacred burial ground;

- Indigenous, Pagan, Hindu, Buddhist, Jehovah's Witness, Evangelical, Atheist, or anything else—

Sometimes those assumptions bring comfort. They link you to generations past. They carry meaning and emotional resonance.

But sometimes... they don't.

What feels right to your parents or community might not be right for you.

And that's okay.

The premise of this book—and of creating your own GoodBye—is this:
You get to do it your way.

Your GoodBye should reflect your values, your beliefs, your life—not someone else's expectation. And the only way that happens is if you make your wishes known.

Understanding Your Options for After-Death Care

Nothing, Embalming, or Cremation?

For some people, this is a huge question. For others, the decision is easy.

I grew up in a culture where embalming was the norm. But after doing my own research, I've chosen cremation for myself. I'm sharing what I've learned—not to convince you—but to help you cut through the myths and make a choice based on facts, values, and your personal comfort level.

Natural or Green Burial

Some individuals, faiths, and cultures prefer quick, simple burials, often within 24 to 48 hours, to avoid decomposition. In these cases, the body is not embalmed but is instead:

- Wrapped in biodegradable cloth,
- Placed in a simple wooden box,
- Or buried directly in the ground.

This is especially common in Jewish and Muslim traditions.

In recent years, natural or green burials have become more popular with environmentally conscious individuals. These burials:

- Avoid toxic chemicals like formaldehyde,
- Do not use burial vaults or grave liners,
- Allow the body to decompose naturally and return to the earth.

Bodies are often buried at shallower depths in green cemeteries, helping the natural process of "dust to dust." Many people find comfort in the idea that their remains can nourish trees, plants, or flowers.

Did you know?

*T*here are green cemeteries in most U.S. states and they are regulated. Traditional cemeteries are less likely to accept a natural burial due to environmental or legal restrictions like sinkholes or toxin concerns.

Natural Burial Pros:

- Minimal environmental impact

- Less invasive to the body
- Lower cost than traditional embalming
- Honoring religious or ethical values

Another form of natural burial is a burial at sea, where the deceased is wrapped in cloth and released into the ocean. This is more than a romantic notion—it's a real, eco-conscious practice that becomes part of the marine ecosystem.

Embalming: What It Is and Why It's Done

Embalming is the process of preserving a body after death. While it's an age-old practice that goes back to ancient Egypt, it became more common in the U.S. during the Civil War. Families wanted fallen soldiers wanted them returned home for burial—which could take time to transport the bodies hundreds of miles.

Benefits of embalming include:

- Slowing body decomposition
- Reducing odor
- Creating a more "presentable" appearance for public viewings
- Allowing more time for funerals and transport, especially across state or national lines

Many cultures and families value this process because it supports rituals of farewell, especially open-casket funerals. Seeing a body at rest can offer comfort and help mourners accept death.

However, if the body was severely injured or deteriorated, an open casket might not be appropriate. In such cases, families often opt for a closed casket with a photo or tribute instead.

The Embalming Process—Not for the Faint of Heart

As a child, I attended viewings with my parents where the deceased looked peaceful—clean, dressed, and hair done. I never questioned how they came to look that way. Much later, I learned how it actually works.

**Warning: The next section is graphic.
You can skip it if you'd rather not know the details.**

There are two types of embalming:

1. Arterial Embalming

    - Blood is drained from the body and replaced with embalming fluid (sometimes colored red to give skin a lifelike tone).
    - This preserves tissues and improves appearance.

1. Cavity Embalming

    - A long, spear-like instrument punctures internal organs (lungs, heart, stomach, intestines, kidneys) to remove fluids and gases.
    - Intestines are often flushed out because pooping after death is common.
    - To ensure the body doesn't leak, morticians typically use:
- Super glue, wires, or cotton in orifices (nose, mouth, anus, genitals)
- Eye caps with spikes to hold eyelids closed
- Lip sewing or gluing
- Makeup and hairstyling to restore a lifelike appearance

In cases where limbs are stiff due to rigor mortis, bodies may need to be forcibly manipulated—sometimes even involving bone breakage.

It's a highly technical and invasive process.

Not everyone is comfortable with it.

Concerns About Embalming

Embalming isn't for everyone. The reasons people avoid it include:

- Cost: Typically $500–$1,000, on top of other funeral expenses that can total $10,000+
- Environmental Impact: Formaldehyde and other chemicals can leach into soil and groundwater
- Religious or Ethical Objections: Some faiths prohibit or discourage altering the body
- Personal Values: Many people feel it's too invasive or artificial

Cremation As A Practical Alternative

Cremation has become increasingly popular as a simpler, often less expensive option.

My former boss told me about his frugal friend whose mother passed away at home. Instead of hiring a funeral service, he loaded her body into his station wagon and drove to the crematorium himself. When he arrived, they told him they couldn't accept her unless she was in a container. So he drove to an appliance store, found an empty refrigerator box, returned, and she was cremated. Her ashes were returned to him in a cardboard box.

Extreme? Maybe. But it proves a point:

Cremation doesn't have to be complicated, expensive, or ceremonial.

You can choose a very simple, direct process—or add as much ritual as you'd like.

Cremation is a common way to handle human remains worldwide.
Simply put, it involves heating the body at a very high temperature until it turns to ashes.
ashes—called "cremains"—can be returned to the family to be buried, kept, or transformed into keepsakes.

The process is straightforward. Bodies are taken to a crematorium where they are usually bathed, cleaned, and dressed, although this isn't required. Most bodies sent for cremation are not embalmed. Jewelry can be removed—or left on if desired. The body must be placed in a container for cremation, which can be a flammable casket, a simple cardboard box, or any combustible container.

The body is then placed in a fire-resistant, brick-lined furnace called a retort. Modern cremation furnaces meet strict environmental and air quality standards and typically use natural gas, propane, or diesel. Temperatures range from 1400 to 2000 degrees Fahrenheit, surrounding the body for up to two hours until it turns to ash. Some large bones don't fully disintegrate and are then ground into fragments or ashes to complete the process.
The cremains are returned to the family in a plastic bag, urn, or container of their choice. What happens next is up to the family—and ideally, reflects the wishes of the person who died. Ashes might be buried in a cemetery, scattered in water, or placed in meaningful locations. The cost of cremation usually ranges from $1,000 to $2,000.

The first cremation I witnessed was in Varanasi, India. Traveling to the Holy River Ganges at dawn was a deeply spiritual experience. The city has 87 ghats—steps leading from the city to the river—where cremations take place daily. Hindus believe the body is a prison for the soul, which is pure and reincarnates after death. Fire is thought to purify sins and free the soul for its next journey. Many come to Varanasi specifically to die, regarded as the holiest city in India. Others are transported there by family, sometimes surrounded by ice to delay decomposition. Well-off families dress the body in orange cloth and marigold flowers. The body is taken on a wooden stretcher to the water's edge, placed on a pyre built from logs, and purified ghee (clarified butter) is poured over it to aid burning. The body burns for at least six hours until only ash remains. Over 100 bodies are cremated at the river each day. For those without family, some bodies are simply released into the river to decompose naturally.

People's wishes about what happens to their ashes vary widely.
Lanee wanted hers buried in her garden.
Tony chose to have his ashes scattered in a special lake.
Mickey wants his ashes released at the peak of his favorite mountain.
Others keep the ashes in urns on a mantle above their fireplace. The options are endless.

Aquamation

Aquamation, also known by names such as water cremation, alkaline hydrolysis, resomation, bio-cremation, green cremation, or flameless cremation, has been around for decades and is becoming a popular alternative to traditional flame cremation.

The process uses water (about 95%) mixed with an alkaline solution (around 5%) to accelerate the natural decomposition of the body. The body is placed on a metal tray inside a pressurized stainless steel chamber. Approximately 80 gallons of water circulate inside, heated to between 200°F and 300°F. Although the water is hot, it doesn't boil due to the pressure. Over 3–4 hours, the body's tissues dissolve into liquid. Remaining bone fragments are dried and pulverized into a powder, which is returned to the family as ashes.

Aquamation is considered to have a lower environmental impact than burial or flame cremation, producing fewer carbon emissions and avoiding toxic chemicals used in embalming. The cost ranges from about $2,000 to $3,500.

In short, you can choose to be buried or cremated. You can opt for a natural, low-intervention farewell, choose embalming to preserve the body, or explore different cremation methods. There are other options too, but these are the most common.

The important thing is — you can choose, but only if you decide ahead of time.

The Casket-Coffin Dilemma

For those who choose traditional burial, a container is needed to hold the body. Unlike cremation or a green burial where a simple cardboard box is often sufficient, most cemeteries have strict rules about what can serve as a final resting place. This opens up a wide range of options—and, unfortunately, lots of pressure on grieving families to spend more than they might want to.

Buying a casket can be overwhelming. Some people plan ahead and pick out their own casket, but most are unprepared and rely heavily on the funeral home staff during a very difficult time.

What's the difference between a casket and a coffin?

A casket is a rectangular box with four sides and a hinged lid.

A coffin has six sides with a removable lid and is tapered to fit the shape of the human body. Though technically different, these terms are often used interchangeably.

For simplicity, I'll use "casket" here, but keep in mind the distinction.

What are caskets made from?

The simplest and least expensive option is a plain pine box—just a box with nothing inside. However, grieving families are often shown a range of deluxe options designed to make them feel as if choosing a bare-bones model means they didn't love their deceased enough. Remember, buying a casket is a commercial transaction aimed at maximizing profit, often by appealing to emotions.

Caskets come in two basic designs:

- Half-couch: The top half of the lid opens for viewings, showing the head and upper body, while the legs remain covered.
- Full-couch: The entire lid opens, typically used when the casket remains closed or there is no viewing.

Caskets are primarily made of metal or wood.

Metal caskets:

Options include gold, copper, and bronze, but these are usually out of reach for most budgets, often costing thousands of dollars. More affordable are steel caskets, available in many colors. For example, my grandmother was laid to rest in a pink steel casket with a plush interior lining and pillow. You can select exterior finishes and interior fabrics to customize your choice. Funeral homes often encourage upselling to heavier steel gauges (e.g., 16-gauge over 18-gauge) because they are more durable—and more expensive. Some metal caskets come with rubber gaskets to help seal out water over time. Stainless steel caskets, which are durable and can be covered with wood veneer for a refined look, are typically pricier. Routine metal caskets average around $2,000, with premium options costing more.

Wooden caskets:

These vary widely by wood type and price. More expensive woods like mahogany, walnut, and cherry are heavier and decompose more slowly, making them more costly and heavier for pallbearers. These are often promoted as the choice "if you really loved them." Mid-range options include oak, maple, and birch. More affordable wooden caskets are made from pine, poplar, or willow—lighter woods that decompose faster. Staining cheaper wood to mimic expensive types is common. For eco-conscious buyers, "green" caskets made from wicker, bamboo, or seagrass provide a natural, biodegradable alternative. Generally, the heavier the wood, the higher the price; the lighter, the cheaper.

Alternative materials:

Because caskets are expensive, many opt for veneer caskets made of pressed wood or fiberboard with a thin wood layer on top. Some fiberboard caskets are covered with heavy cloth, while laminate caskets are plastic but designed to look like wood.

Where can you buy a casket?

Don't feel limited to the funeral home's offerings—they often push items they want to clear from inventory. You have many options:

- Purchase ahead of time and have the casket shipped to your home or funeral home.
- Online retailers like Titan Caskets, Casket Royale, Direct Caskets, and Batesville Caskets offer a wide selection.
- You can even buy caskets from Walmart or Amazon.
- For unexpected deaths, companies like Overnight Caskets can deliver your choice quickly.

Design and personalization

If you want a casket that truly reflects the person, many companies offer themed or customizable designs. For example, Titan Caskets sells military-style caskets for veterans. Expression Coffins offers a variety of artistic themes—animals, cars and motorcycles, comic characters, flowers, hobbies, landmarks, patriotic motifs, religious symbols, sports themes, and even outer space designs. You can even create custom caskets with photos or favorite imagery. For motorcycle enthusiasts, Harley Davidson caskets exist. The casket industry encourages personal style—go in style and do it your way.

But wait—there's more!

Choosing a casket is just the start. To be buried in a cemetery, you may also need to purchase a burial vault or grave liner.

But that's a whole other conversation.

Burial Vaults or Grave Liners

Buying a coffin doesn't necessarily guarantee you can be buried in it—many cemeteries require an additional outer container called a burial vault or grave liner. These containers fit around the coffin when it's lowered into the ground. Most people don't realize this requirement until the time of burial. While state laws might not mandate them, cemetery rules often do.

What's their purpose?

An external burial container supports the weight of the soil around the grave, preventing the coffin from being crushed or the ground from sinking over time. A grave liner is typically made of reinforced concrete and usually has no bottom. A burial vault, on the other hand, is a sealed enclosure that fully protects the coffin.

Once buried, these containers help keep the ground level, which prevents people from tripping, stops tombstones from tipping over, and makes lawn maintenance easier for cemetery staff. Note that while burial vaults protect the coffin better than grave liners, neither stops the natural process of decomposition.

Costs:

- Grave liners: $500 to $1,400 (liners without a base tend to be less expensive)
- Burial vaults: $1,000 to $4,000 or more

When planning your burial expenses, be sure to factor in the cost of these containers!

Tombstones

You can be buried without a marker or tombstone—it's not required, and some people choose not to have one.

However, in many cultures and regions, placing a tombstone or grave marker is customary to help people locate the grave. Cremated remains may also be marked if buried in a cemetery.

Cemeteries usually have rules about tombstones, regulating aspects such as size, material, height, design, and inscriptions. Flat stones generally cost between $500 and $5,000, while granite or marble tombstones can range from a few thousand dollars to over $15,000 or $20,000.

Funeral homes and cemeteries often encourage purchasing larger, upright stones, claiming they make visiting easier—though this can also be a way to upsell grieving families.
You might want a colorful tombstone with pictures, sayings, or designs that reflect your personality and legacy.

Keep in mind, though, cemeteries have guidelines about what's allowed. And if you consider burial outside a cemetery, local laws and town ordinances may restrict where bodies can be buried. No matter where or when, there are always rules to navigate.

Objects Made Out of Ashes

Choosing cremation is just the beginning—what happens to your ashes afterward can vary widely, and transactions among those handling your remains often determine their final resting place unless you specify your wishes.

Most people have their ashes placed in bags or urns. Cemeteries generally don't mind whether you're buried in a coffin or an urn, but you must be in something.

Scattering ashes in a cemetery typically requires prior permission. The biggest legal challenges arise when scattering ashes in nature, because laws vary by location.

Legal Restrictions:

Laws about scattering ashes depend on your state or locality. For example, Florida has no state-wide rules but local restrictions may apply; California has stricter regulations.

- Scattering ashes in your own yard is usually allowed.
- National forests prohibit scattering.
- State and local parks may or may not allow it—check with authorities.
- Ashes can be scattered at sea, but only at least three miles offshore in deep water.
- It is illegal to scatter ashes in inland waters like rivers, lakes, or streams.

- **Urns and Containers:**
  Urns come in countless forms—stone, pottery, painted, or custom sculptures shaped like animals, motorcycles, or decorated with faces and cultural symbols. A friend once painted her late husband's urn with an image of him fishing, honoring his passion.

- **Jewelry and Keepsakes:**
  A popular way to keep loved ones close is through ash jewelry. Ashes can be placed in lockets, pendants, beads for bracelets, or rings. Some companies claim to create diamonds from ashes, though industry standards question the quality.

- **Art and Decorative Items:**
  Ashes can be mixed with glass to create art pieces like lamps, stained glass windows, or ornaments. Some families have Christmas ornaments made from ashes. Ashes can also be combined with ceramics or stone to form sculptures, including lifelike busts.
- **Pet Memorials:**
  Pet crematoriums offer to craft ashes into statues or keepsakes. One facility offers a variety of items to keep pets close at home.
- **Ashes Turned to Stones:**
  Ashes can be processed into stone-like memorials, often shared among mourners. Prices vary by animal type:
    - Dog ashes stones: ~$995
    - Cat ashes stones: ~$800
    - Horse ashes stones: ~$10,000
    - Small pets like hamsters or birds: ~$700
    - Humans can be made into 40–80 stones for about $2,500.
- **Unique and Surreal Uses:**
  Entrepreneurs have found creative ways to incorporate ashes into items such as:
    - Stuffed toys
    - Paint for pictures of the deceased
    - Picture frames made with ashes
    - Tattoos incorporating ashes
    - Pencils made from cremated remains (about 240 pencils per body), often engraved with the deceased's name
    - Vinyl records pressed with the loved one's voice
    - Urns designed to grow trees from ashes

What you can do with ashes is endless.

My student told about how her brother's ashes were turned into a hash pipe that the family smoked out of at his memorial service.

Ed Headrick, the Frisbee inventor, requested his ashes be mixed into plastic for Frisbees to share with family and friends.

Hunters have had ashes embedded in ammunition, so each bullet contains a small amount of ashes.

Letting People Know You're Gone

When someone dies, it's important to let friends, family, colleagues, and acquaintances know. But how do you do that?

Many people today post announcements on social media platforms like Facebook. But what if you don't use social media? Not everyone relies on electronic communication, and the old telephone books are long gone.

While most people have cell phones, tracking down numbers without prior knowledge is nearly impossible.

Historically, people relied on newspaper obituaries.

Here are some questions to consider:

- Do you want an obituary?
- If yes, where would you like it published?
- Would you like a photo included? If so, pick one and let others know which photo to use. Some prefer a recent picture; others may want an image from younger days.
- Would you like to write your own obituary?
- Or would you prefer someone else to write it? If so, who?

I used to think that newspapers automatically publish obituaries for free, like they do for celebrities or public figures. But for most people, families have to pay for obituary notices. The cost depends on length and can range from around $100 to over $1,000.

What do you want in your obituary?

It's a good idea to draft your obituary now, so others can edit it later if needed. You know details that others won't—and once you're gone, they can't ask you!

- Who should be mentioned? Usually spouses, parents, and children are listed. But what about previous spouses, especially if someone was married multiple times? Sometimes new spouses omit earlier marriages or family members. It's good to be clear on what you want.
- Are there associations or groups that should be informed? You might belong to clubs, professional organizations, religious groups, or volunteer networks that would want to know. These groups typically don't charge to publish announcements and will appreciate knowing.

To summarize, consider:

- Which newspapers should carry your obituary?
- Which social media platforms should have announcements?
- What about workplaces, professional associations, civic groups, religious or spiritual organizations?
- Don't forget schools you attended, or musical, recreational, or sports groups.

Make a list of these contacts and share it with someone you trust. People care about you and will want to know when you're gone—even if you don't expect it.

Distribution of Your "Stuff"

We spend a lifetime collecting material objects.
will happen to all the things you've accumulated over the years?
Who do you want to have what?
This a topic that often causes disputes after someone passes away. It's important to be clear about who gets what.

Most of our stuff might not truly matter to us. Some people are materialistic control-freaks; others couldn't care less about objects. But usually, there are some items that do hold meaning. These might be things you want to stay in the family, go to certain friends, or be cherished in a special way. It can be painful to see these items sold at a yard sale or tossed out, simply because people don't realize their emotional significance.

People won't know unless you tell them!

For example, I have a set of little glasses that belonged to my great-grandmother. To some, they're just pretty glasses, nothing more. To me, they are precious relics, tied to a story, a time, and a place — and to someone I never met. I also have a wooden sideboard that belonged to my auntie. Over the years, she painted it layers of blue, white, pink, and brown. I spent **hours** stripping off the paint to reveal the natural wood beneath. That piece is dear to me, and I want it to stay in the family. A cousin inherited some of auntie's expensive antiques meant to be kept in the family — but she quickly sold them at auction. This made my auntie sad and angered family members who had hoped to keep them. While objects are just things, there are some that I hope will be saved by my loved ones as remembrances.

Take some time to look through your belongings. Consider doing a Marie Kondo-style decluttering: get rid of things you don't care about and keep what is useful or brings you joy. Your relatives will thank you later when they come to clear out your house. I know many hoarders whose homes are overflowing with papers, clothes, and objects that have little real meaning — leaving a huge mess for others to sort through.

One type of item that often causes family conflict is **photographs.** Digital photos are easy to copy and share, but old paper photographs are often one-of-a-kind and can lead to intense emotional reactions if some people keep them and don't share.

What other belongings do you have that are important to you? Who should have them to remember you by?

Typical Funeral Swag and Other Miscellaneous Costs

At funerals or memorial services, families often choose to give small items of remembrance to those who attend. Think of these as "swag" — something we all get – where everyone receives something as a keepsake.

A whole industry has been built around producing and promoting these items, encouraging families to include them as part of a meaningful farewell.

Each item comes with a cost, which depends on the type of item and the quantity purchased. These costs can range from minimal to quite expensive. As mentioned earlier, some people even have their loved one's ashes turned into memorial stones that guests can take home — what they do with those stones is anyone's guess!

Here are some commonly distributed types of funeral swag and associated costs:

- **Pamphlets or Booklets:** These describe the life and accomplishments of the deceased. They can be a simple single sheet or a more elaborate booklet with color photos and a sturdy cover. Costs vary depending on design, number of pages, and quantity printed.
- **Balloons**: Traditionally released to symbolize the soul's ascent, balloons have fallen out of favor because they break and litter the environment, posing risks to wildlife. Not a very kind way to celebrate someone's life.
- **Bubbles:** A popular eco-friendly substitute for balloons, guests might be given small containers of bubbles to blow skyward — symbolizing the soul rising. Large bubble-making devices can also add a playful, joyful element to the ceremony.
- **Doves:** It used to be common to release doves at funerals. My mom told stories of her brother who brought caged doves that would be released at a precise moment — the birds were trained to return home and reused at multiple funerals. However, this practice is now discouraged as it's stressful for the birds. Instead, folded origami paper doves are often handed out as a humane alternative.
- **Flower Seeds or Bulbs**: Guests may receive packets of seeds or bulbs to plant in a special place. Plants growing symbolize life continuing and spreading — a beautiful metaphor for how the deceased's impact endures. Forget-me-nots are a common choice.
- **Candy:** Sweet treats featuring the departed's favorite candy can bring smiles and remind people to savor life's sweetness.
- **Candles:** Often given out and lit as people offer prayers or kind words. The flame symbolizes life and spirit. Sometimes candles are ceremonially extinguished together, signifying that the departed's light has gone out. (A quick caution: be careful holding lit candles near hair or clothing, as I saw a woman's long hair go up in flames when someone held their candle too close!)

- **Flowers:** Funeral flowers have a long tradition. Originally, their fragrance masked the odor of decay and lifted spirits. A single floral vase can cost around $100, and coffin sprays several hundred dollars. Flowers are usually left at the gravesite until they wilt, then removed. Some families substitute lasting memorials like wind chimes or personalized blankets with inscriptions such as "Beloved Father" to avoid the expense and waste.
- **Photos:** Displaying photos of the deceased at wakes, funerals, or memorials is now standard. These range from framed portraits to elaborate, professionally designed displays or simple poster boards with handwritten notes.
- **Videos:** Photo slideshows set to music have become popular ways to celebrate a life. These can be homemade or professionally produced, often involving significant costs. Funeral homes may offer videographer services, but at a price.
- **Music:** Music is essential in most memorials. It may be played softly in the background, include the deceased's favorite songs, or feature traditional religious hymns like *Amazing Grace*. Live soloists, organists, or pianists can add elegance, while pre-recorded music requires a good sound system. Some funerals include bagpipers or buglers playing military taps. The style and scale of music can vary widely, reflecting the tone the family wishes to set — from solemn to celebratory. Music is a key part of the funeral industry, and while it costs money, it often brings comfort and meaning.
- **Food and Drink:** Providing sustenance is crucial at wakes or visitations, where family and friends may be present for hours. A post-burial meal is common, whether at a religious center, a home, a veterans' hall, a rented venue, or a restaurant. Food at memorial services serves a symbolic role as well. Offering an elegant spread sends a message of care and gratitude to mourners, while a simple bowl of chips might be perceived as indifferent.

Food choices can set the tone of the gathering and honor the departed's memory.

There's more!

Funeral Transaction Costs and the Funeral Industrial Complex

When planning a funeral, it's important to remember there will be many people involved who expect to be compensated — either directly or indirectly. These include:

- The mortician and funeral home staff
- Office personnel
- Custodians who clean before and after the service
- Hearse driver
- Limo or bus drivers for family transportation (if used)
- Pallbearers
- Cemetery workers who dig the grave and cover the body afterward
- Vendors for any special additions such as horse-drawn carriages or dove releases
- In some cultures, hired mourners who attend to show how popular and beloved the deceased was

Beyond these, there are travel expenses such as plane and car transportation for out-of-town guests, hotel stays, meals, and other related costs.

Another often overlooked expense is perpetual care. If buried in a cemetery, the grounds will require ongoing maintenance — grass will need to be cut, gravestones may need to be straightened if they tilt, and other upkeep costs may arise. Even in death, there are costs simply for "being somewhere."

Feeling overwhelmed? You should be. Dying is expensive — though **it doesn't have to be.**

The funeral industry is a complex duality. On one hand, it provides vital support to grieving families, helping them navigate loss and focus on mourning. Think of it as a kind of public health and social service.

On the other hand, this industry also capitalizes on grief, presenting an image of care while profiting from it. This "funeral industrial complex" is estimated to be a $20 billion industry in the U.S. alone.

Based on my research, here are some ballpark figures to give you an idea of what you might spend if you choose to use these services. Some costs are unavoidable, while others come down to personal choice:

- These estimates are rough and vary widely — prices may be significantly higher or lower depending on your location and preferences. More often, they tend to be higher.

These are financial estimates for an embalming type of burial and funeral:

Funeral director and staff services	$3000
Transfer of deceased person to the funeral home	$400
Embalming	$1000
Preparing the body for showing	$500
Funeral home use and staff costs for viewing	$700
Funeral home use and staff for funeral	$800
Coach, bus, limo, van	$1000
Printed materials	$250

Casket	$2500
Grave liner	$1000
Burial vault	$3000
Obituary	$500
Music	$300
Clergy	$500
Tombstone	$400
Swag	$500
Food	$1000
Perpetual care	$300
Photos, video display	$600
Hotels	?
Plane, car, parking, etc.	?
Rough Estimate (no fringes)	$18250

I looked online at funeral home costs and different websites and some of them come in closer to $10,000. However, they don't include some of the items above. Also, it must be noted that cremations will cost less since they do not require embalming, a casket, grave liner, or vault. As listed in this chapter, there are a bunch of other thing that you could purchase for your GoodBye.

The thing that you have to sort out is if you are going to spend ten to twenty thousand dollars or more, is this the way you want to spend it?

What else could you do with that money for yourself or for those you leave behind instead of giving it to the funeral industrial complex?

It's your money.
It's your life. It's your death.
It's your choice what you do with it all.

9

Making A GoodBye For You and Others

Making A Good GoodBye For You and Others

Death as a Final Transactional Relationship

Death, like life, is a transactional relationship.

We impact one another in countless ways — consciously and unconsciously — and how we choose to die is our last chance to shape a meaningful relationship.

For all the good connections we have made throughout our lives, dying offers a final opportunity to give thanks.

is a moment to let others know we love them, to express gratitude for the gifts they have given us, both big and small.

For all the ways we wish we had done better, this is our chance to make amends.

Many of us carry decades of hurt and anger in our hearts and on our shoulders.

It's time to release that weight, so we can fly free.

Throughout life, we have learned some profound truths:

- We are more than our bodies.
- We are more than our jobs, careers, or accomplishments.
- We hold knowledge that no one else has.
- We feel emotions that remain unseen by others.
- We have experienced adventures and moments that no one else will ever know.
- We are far more than others perceive.

We are miracles of life, deserving to be celebrated simply for being here.

We have done many good things.
We have made mistakes — some of them big.
We should be loved despite the mistakes and forgiven for our failures.

Like a child learning to walk, who must fall many times before mastering the steps.

Our mistakes teach us how to walk, run, and dance through life.

Sometimes it takes many attempts before we get it right. As the saying goes,

> **"If it takes 1,000 whacks of the reed to break the rock, the first 999 were necessary."**

Breaking free from the need to please others is not easy.

Breaking away from customs, traditions, and societal expectations — about how we should live and how we should die — can be even harder.

But once we decide to do things our own way, we can experience liberation.

As singer Jimmy Cliff sings in *I Can See Clearly Now*, once we free ourselves from others' expectations, a clearer, lighter path emerges.

Customs and traditions around death vary widely by culture and family. Memorial ceremonies and funerals offer communities a chance to say goodbye and grieve together.

In some cultures, dying is a natural family and community event — children witness death and learn early that it is an inevitable part of being human.

Today, however, **death is often a taboo subject**, rarely discussed openly.
People are frequently hidden away in hospitals or hospice facilities, dying under the care of strangers.

The modern approach makes death scarier than it needs to be, cloaking it in fear and avoidance.

Some psychologists argue we need what they call "terror management therapy" — a way to help us become more comfortable with death as the inevitable transition it is.

How Can You Craft Your GoodBye Party to Deliver a Message?

Your farewell celebration is your final opportunity to tell your story.

What message do you want to leave behind?

Most of us wish our send-off to be joyous — uplifting the hearts of those we love so we can be set free into the sky. We want laughter to echo as people recall the funny moments we shared. We want stories of adventures, challenges overcome, and the love we tried to share every day of our lives. Instead of black clothes and tears of sorrow, we hope for smiles and joyful tears as we begin our next great adventure.

As singer LeeAnn Womack reminds us in her song *I Hope You Dance*, and as the film *Flashdance* shows, we can dance through life — even through the hardest times.

We are blessed to share this precious moment in time, here together — breathing, feeling joy and gratitude for each new day, each person who has touched our lives, and whom we have touched in return. We have loved. We have laughed. We have cried. We have suffered. And we have survived immense traumas, often known only to ourselves.

Our external self is what others see. Friends, family, and colleagues may think they know us well, but few truly know the real us.

Sometimes, we struggle to understand who we really are, why we are here, and what the meaning of our life has been.

A GoodBye is our chance to make sure that others know OUR STORY.

If we have lived well, it sets the stage for a peaceful and meaningful farewell.

If we feel our lives are incomplete, this is the time to make amends and try to heal the wounds we carry — and also to repair the hurts we may have caused others.

Would you like to design your own GoodBye?

I do. I am.

It's perfectly OK to design your own rituals to help you move into grief — and eventually, move out of it.

In some traditions, mourners stay at home, where visitors stop by to bring food, flowers, or offer prayers.

Some people choose to remain at home for days, weeks, or even months, processing the transition in their own time.

Many want a funeral; others don't want anything. Some desire a huge party with all the music and trimmings.

The point is — **you get to decide.**

Long ago, people died at home and were mourned by their community.

But in the 20th century, a complex industry around death emerged. Death at home was replaced by hospitals and medical facilities.

This isn't all bad — there are many resources hospitals and hospices provide that make dying less painful and more humane for everyone involved.

When my pony was dying, I begged the veterinarian to do what she could to save him. She gave him loving care, but at some point she looked me straight in the eye and said, "I can't cure old." There's a limit to our lifespan, and no matter what health professionals do, sometimes they can't stop the inevitable.

Turning death into a financial transaction has led to "care" that's profit-centered instead of human-centered. The body itself becomes a commodity. The funeral industrial complex leaves little room for direct, meaningful family involvement, robbing us of the chance to create our own rituals and hands-on engagement.

GoodBye seeks to empower *you* to take charge of your life — and your death arrangements.

- Have courage.
- Be brave.
- Talk openly about the elephant in the room — the subject everyone tiptoes around but few address.

For those of us who have spent our lives avoiding difficult conversations for fear of upsetting others, here's a truth: **It won't matter anymore**. So what if they get mad? Dying offers a rare opportunity to speak your truth.

What if you're avoiding talking about death because it might make others sad? By showing that you are comfortable discussing dying honestly and openly, you help ease their burden. You can cry together. Talking may help both of you accept things as they are. As the weight lifts, a lightness may follow — allowing laughter, and a deeper, truer love. That is a gift beyond measure.

Years ago, I met Dr. Elisabeth Kübler-Ross, whose work on death and dying changed the way we understand loss. What she shared that has always stayed with me:

Sometimes people wait to die until no one is around.

They pass in the still of night, or when loved ones step out for a moment.

She believed this is not coincidence.

That sometimes we hold on as long as we can because of the love we feel.

And we can only let go when we're alone—when there's no one left to hold us back.

We stay because we love and are loved.

But what if something wonderful awaits us?

The GoodBye Letter

Maybe you want to consider writing a GoodBye letter to be read at your funeral or memorial service.

Perhaps you want to write a series of letters to specific people in your life.

Sometimes, it's too hard to say the things we want face-to-face.

Writing gives you time to think, reflect, and choose your words carefully.

Who would you like to have your say with? Here are some common types of letters you might consider:

For parents:

What would you like to say to your children as you leave this earth? If you have multiple children, you have a unique relationship with each one. You've witnessed their struggles and successes. You love them all

— but you love them differently. As parents, we sometimes upset or disappoint our children. Your letter could explain why, and ask for their understanding — and forgiveness. This may be the last thing they have of you, something they may read again and again. Make it sweet. Make it kind. Make it honest. Give them your gift of everlasting love.

For children:

If you might die before your parents do, what do you want them to know? They know a lot about you, but not everything — your hidden thoughts, your feelings, your dreams. You may have anger, regrets, or sadness to share. It's important that those most important to us truly know who we are. And you can also include your wishes for your body or legacy, should you pass before them. It's never too early to write this GoodBye letter — and you can always update it later.

For friends:

Friends have journeyed with us — sharing fun times, secrets, travels, and support. They would appreciate knowing your thoughts and gratitude. You probably have stories that will make them smile and laugh. Let them know how their companionship made your life's road easier and richer.

For lovers:

There have likely been many — lifelong partners, soul mates, secret lovers, or unrequited loves. Some loved us deeply; some have been disappointing and some have made our soul sing, while some may have broken our hearts. It's okay to tell them how they affected you. Let that special someone know you truly loved them, or express the wishes you held in your heart. Tell the one that got away that you cared. Tell the one you ran away from why. As you think of all those you cared about, there's likely much to say to each.

For colleagues:

Work relationships shape us. Some helped you build your career; others may have caused harm. Maybe you never spoke your truth to either group. As you prepare to leave, perhaps you want to say your peace.

Our love letters will be cherished. People may hold them in their hearts and minds forever, so be careful what you say.

Letters that acknowledge unkindness can clear the air and may even help those who hurt us to change, so others don't have to suffer as we did.

For those we want to confront and call out, it's often better they don't see these letters until after we're gone.
They may need to know they've been mean jerks, but wait until you are gone to tell them so, since some people can be unkind to the very end.

Writing what you can't say in life may bring you relief.
These letters give you your final say.

It's wise to store them securely — perhaps in a locked box, with your lawyer, or a trusted friend who will release them after you pass.

Don't leave them where they can be read early.

You deserve your privacy and dignity.

Or maybe, you want to go to your grave holding your secrets, feelings, and knowledge close inside.

You don't have to share if you don't want to.
It's your choice.

After all, this is your final opportunity to do things your way.

I hope you find this book to be helpful. It is my gift to you.
Maybe we will meet up sometime, some way, some day.

You never know…

10

Words of Wisdom

Parting Wisdom: Words to Guide the Journey

On Creating Life and Legacy

"The best way to predict the future is to create it." — Peter Drucker

"We all die. The goal isn't to live forever, the goal is to create something that will." — Chuck Palahniuk

"A ship in harbor is safe, but that is not what ships are built for." — John A. Shedd

"A smooth sea never made a skilled sailor." — Franklin D. Roosevelt

"Every exit is an entry somewhere else." — Tom Stoppard

On Living Fully and Courageously

"It is not death that a man should fear, but he should fear never beginning to live." — Marcus Aurelius

"Some people die at 25 and aren't buried until 75." — Benjamin Franklin

"I would rather die a meaningful death than to live a meaningless life." — Corazon Aquino

"Courage is not the absence of fear, but rather the judgment that something else is more important than fear." — Ambrose Redmoon

"To die will be an awfully big adventure." — Peter Pan

On Death as Part of Life

"Death is not the opposite of life, but a part of it." — Haruki Murakami

"Death ends a life, not a relationship." — Mitch Albom

"Tell your friend that in his death, a part of you dies and goes with him. Wherever he goes, you also go. He will not be alone." — Jiddu Krishnamurti

"Death is a challenge. It tells us not to waste time... It tells us to tell each other right now that we love each other." — Leo Buscaglia

"I hope it is true that a man can die and yet not only live in others but give them life, and not only life, but that great consciousness of life." — Jack Kerouac

On Leadership and Facing the Storm

"The pessimist complains about the wind; the optimist expects it to change; the realist adjusts the sails." — William Arthur Ward

"The true test of a captain is how they navigate through the storm, not during calm waters." — Anonymous

"A captain is not defined by their rank or position but by their actions and character." — Anonymous

"The strength of the captain lies in their ability to inspire and empower their crew." — Anonymous

"A successful captain is one who can adapt to changing tides and steer their ship toward new horizons." — Anonymous

On Bravery and the Final Journey

"If we must die, we die defending our rights." — Sitting Bull

"When your time comes to die... sing your death song, and die like a hero going home." — Tecumseh

"I've told my children that when I die, to release balloons in the sky to celebrate that I graduated. For me, death is a graduation." — Elisabeth Kübler-Ross

Go forward into your next great adventure.
Be curious.
Be brave.
With love in your heart.
Discover the magic
Inside
and to what awaits.
Be open to all the possibilities of who you were meant to be.
And could still be.

11

It's About You Workbook

It's About YOU:

Your Own Personal GoodBye Celebration and Transformation Workbook

In this Workbook to go with GOODBYE, take time to answer the questions posed in the next pages.

Everyone will benefit if you do.

Especially YOU.

12

Who Have You Been?

Who Have You Been?

People may know bits and pieces about you. It will be useful for you to reflect upon your journey until now. This information may also be helpful for others to know. Here are some questions that will help you to think about Who Have You Been?

When were you born?

What day and year?

Where were you born?

Who was your mother?

Who was your father?

What is your social security number?

Tell about any siblings you may have had.

Who took care of you before you were old enough to go to school?

Where did you go to elementary school? (Kindergarten – 5th Grade)

Where did you go to middle school? (Grades 5-8)

Where did you go to secondary or high school? (Grades 9-12)

Did you go to any vocational training?

Did you go to college? If so, where did you go and what did you study?

Did you graduate? If so, what was your degree?

What are some of the things you wanted to do when you became an adult?

Did you make some of those dreams come true?

What do you think are words that best describe who you have been?

What have been some of your greatest fears and worries?

What other things do you think people should know about who you have been?

13

Your Family Tree

Your Family Tree

Some families have created detailed logs of who is related to us throughout the generations while others of us don't have very good records at all. Perhaps there is one person in your family who kept records but for whatever reason those records get lost or not shared with you. For generations to come, see if you can fill in the family tree chart below.

Start with yourself and fill in your mom and dad's information. Then talk about your grandparents, and great-grandparents if you can. If you know where and when they were born and the dates when they died and where they are buried, that information could be helpful to others. Include stories about what you know about as many of your relatives that you can. You know things about them that probably no one else knows. You've heard stories, you've had interactions and experiences - share them! What did they look like? Where did they live? What was their personality? Stories like this matter, to us and to future generations who'd like to learn more about where they came from.

MOM's Side

DAD's Side

14

Your Jobs and Military Experience

Talk about your Jobs and Military Experience

Many of us gain a sense of identity – and money – from the kinds of jobs that we have held. Some jobs are with us serving as volunteers, perhaps at a museum, park, or civic organization. Most of us have had paid jobs throughout our life. They may have started when we were young as we babysat or cut grass; over time we probably have held many different jobs where we earned money. Some of us have spent large amounts of our life working for the government or military organizations. The exercise outlined in this chapter is for you to reflect upon all of those jobs and experiences and what they have meant for you. Probably few people besides yourself know the full range of what you have done. Have fun reflecting and writing about them!

What was your FIRST job?

List as many of the jobs that you've had that you can remember.

What was your favorite or best job? Why?

What was your least favorite job? Why?

Was there a job or career that you wanted that you didn't get a chance to pursue? Tell about it.

Do you have any military experience?   Yes   No

If you did, where did you serve?

What are your military credentials?

What was your unit information?

Who were some of your military friends or leaders?

What does having served in the military mean to you?

Did you work for the government or serve your country in other ways? Tell about what you did.

15

Your Hobbies, Sports, and Recreation

We are not just workaholics. We have a life of our own in which we choose to do interesting things. We use our time and money to have hobbies, play sports, video games, make music, sing, create art, act or help in theatrical performances, gamble, collect objects, or engage in countless other types of activities. These recreational options may be some of our favorite things. What have been the ways that you have spent your discretionary time?

What have been your favorite things to do for fun?

Do you/did you play any sports? Talk about them!

What kinds of hobbies did you have?

What have been your favorite types of recreation? Tell about them.

If you have any down-time, how do you like to spend it?

What have been your favorite TV shows?

What are your favorite movies?

Who are your favorite bands?

What are your favorite songs?

What are your favorite games?

Tell more about your things like these that you have done that have brought you pleasure.

16

Your Relationships

In this section of your Workbook, take some time to think about the most important relationships in your life. Some of these, hopefully, have been loving and pleasant ones. There may be some relationships that you have had that have not been very pleasant, but they have been a major influence in your life. You are given some broad categories of people, and then plenty of blank space to write more about them or about other relationships that have impacted who you are and how your life has turned out.

Who are you closest to in your family? Why?

Who are you least close to in your family? Why?

What words describe your mother? What was she like?

What words describe your father? What was he like?

Who are your best friend(s)?

Who was your first sweetheart?

Do you want to talk about other people you have dated or been sweet on?

Who have been the most important intimate relationships in your life?

Did you marry or have a long-term relationship with somebody(s)? Who? How long did those relationships last?

Who has been the major love of your life?

Do you have any children? If so, talk about who they are and your relationship with them?

Did you have any neighbors that impacted your life? Who and how?

Did you have any teachers or mentors that impacted your life? Who and how?

Who are the most important people to you in your life?

17

Pets and Animals

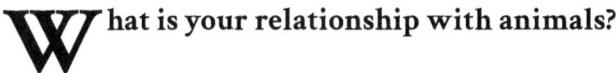hat is your relationship with animals?

Some people consider animals to be their family members. Other people have never had any pets. Some people do not like animals. This section is for you to talk about your relationship with 4-legged, winged, scaly, of swimming animals.

Have you had any pets? Tell about them!

Cats

Dogs

Birds

Fish

Rabbits

Hamsters, guinea pigs, etc.

Reptiles, lizards, snakes, etc.

Horses

Farm animals (cows, goats, pigs, etc).

Nature animals - Deer, otters, bears. Etc.

Other animal friends

What animals do you not like or are scared of?

What animals or pets have been your favorite?

Talk more if you wish about your relationship with animals.

18

Where Have You Lived?

Where have you have lived?

Some of us are born, live, and die in the same town. Others of us have lived many places. Where we have lived, the kinds of homes we've had, and what happened in them all impact who we have become. Tell more about where you have lived.

Where were you born?

Where did you grow up?

How many places did you live before you turned age 18? Where were they?

Where have you lived since you were 18? List as many towns and places as you can remember.

What has been your favorite place to live and why?

What have been some of the challenges where you have lived?

What is your dream home like?

Tell more about what home means to you.

19

Your Travels

Your Travels

Most people travel and our travels shape our adventures and the way we see the world. Some of us travel to places close to home while others of us travel great distances, even to other lands and countries. Reflect upon your traveling adventures and what they have meant to you.

What are your favorite "close to home" places that you like to go?

What states have you traveled to?

List the countries that you have traveled to.

Where have you gone on vacation?

What has been your favorite place to visit?

Where would you like to travel to one day if you get the chance?

What else would you like to share about your travels?

20

Who Are You Now?

Who Are You Now?

Who we are today is not necessarily who we have been in the past. Sometimes we seem frozen in people's minds about who we were years ago. We change! Here are some questions that may help others to better understand who you are now.

Where are you living now?

Who are you living with?

Are you employed? If so, doing what?

Are you retired? If so, from what?

Do you volunteer or do any civic work? If so, what is it?

What do you like to do in your spare time?

Who are your best friends now?

What is your health like?

Who are your doctors?

    Names

Contact information

Do you give permission to any of your family to talk with them?
    Yes   No

If you can't make your own healthcare decisions, who do you want to make them?

    Name
    Contact information

Do you have a living will?   Yes   No

Do you want to donate any of your organs if you die? Yes No

If you have a health condition from which you may not recover, do you want to be kept alive through use of medical interventions?   Yes No

What other information would you like to share about you and your life at this point in time?

21

Your Religious or Spiritual Life

What are your religious or spiritual views?

Religion and spirituality can be important for people, especially as we contemplate dying. This section of questions gives you an opportunity to think about its importance to you and what role you would like it to have in your future funeral, memorial services, or how you want people to honor your legacy.

Did you grow up in any particular religion?   Yes   No

If so, what was it?

Do you practice any particular religion or spiritual orientation today? If so, tell about it.

What or who is God to you? Does a spiritual orientation guide you in your life? If so, tell about it.

Is there a particular clergy person you want to be present or say words at your funeral or memorial service?   Yes   No

If yes, who is it?

What is their contact information?

If there are particular religious or spiritual rituals, words, or activities that you would like at your funeral or memorial service, please tell us about what you would like.

What other ways would you like to incorporate a spiritual presence in your transition?

22

When You Die

What do you want to do with your body when you die?

When we die, somebody must do something with our body. What is that something, and who is that somebody? While this may not be the most comfortable thing to think or talk about, it is necessary.

Do you want to have an autopsy performed on your body after you die?
    Yes   No

What funeral home would you like your body to be taken to?

    Name

    Town or contact information

Do you want to be

Embalmed	Yes	No
Cremated	Yes	No
Natural burial	Yes	No

Other? Explain.

Do you have certain clothes that you would like to wear when you are embalmed, cremated, or buried? If so, please state what you would like to wear.

Are there any particular object(s) that you would like to go with you when you are embalmed, cremated, or buried? Please say what it is.

Do you want your body to be put into:

A casket   Yes   No

If yes, what type? (See GoodBye for a list of options)

An urn   Yes   No

Do you have one picked out?   Yes   No

If yes, where is it?

If not, what type of container would you like your ashes put in?

What other information would you like to share about what you want done with your body and container?

23

Burial Questions

Where do you want your remains to go?

We all have to go somewhere when we die. Where do you want your remains to go? Here is a list to choose from.

Do you want to be buried in a cemetery?

What cemetery and where?

Do you have a plot already? If so, please specify the details, plot number, contact person:

Is there a family plot or section near the burial of others that you would like to near?   Yes   No

If yes, who are their names and where are they located?

Do you have casket, burial liner or vault preferences?

Ashes

Do you want your ashes to be spread in a particular location(s)?   Yes   No

Where? Be as detailed as possible so people know.

Do you want your ashes transformed into objects, like jewelry, stones, or other objects? If so, please specify what you would like your ashes to be turned into and then where you would like them to go or who to be given to (See GoodBye for a list of options).

Do you want your remains put into a mausoleum or in a vault in a particular building or park location?   Yes   No

If yes, please identify where and whether you already have made these arrangements:

Do you want a tombstone or marker?

> Yes, I have one picked out (please tell more about it)
> Yes, but I don't have one picked out
> Yes, I am entitled to a veteran's marker
> No, I don't want one

If you have ideas of what you want for a marker or stone, please tell about it.

What other information would you like to share about where you would like your remains to go?

24

Your Memorial Preferences

What kind of funeral or memorial do you want?

When people die, it is customary to hold a family or public ceremony that honors their life and celebrates their transition. Many funerals or memorials are designed in a way that the funeral home recommends to the grieving family. Other events are constructed around traditions, customs, religious requirements, or what the family wants. Some people do not want any memorial service at all. If you don't want a service, then let people know. If you do, then let people know what you would like it to be. It is the position of the GOODBYE model of death transition that YOU SHOULD GET TO CHOOSE WHAT KIND OF GOODBYE CELEBRATION THAT YOU WANT.

Do you want to have some sort of funeral or memorial service to celebrate your life?

Yes   No   I don't care

Who would you like to speak at your funeral/memorial service?

Clergy member

Family member(s)

Friends

Where would you like to have your service?

At the funeral home	Yes	No
At a religious building	Yes	No
At the cemetery	Yes	No
Place where my ashes were put	Yes	No
At my home	Yes	No
I don't care where	Yes	No

In a particular building: Specify where.

In a particular outdoor location: Specify where.

Do you want any particular type of flowers at your service?
Yes   No

If so, what kind are your favorites?

Most people prefer some particular readings, poems, or holy words read at their services. If you would, please say what they are so they can be read.

Do you want any particular type of music played?

Yes   No   None

Please specify if you want certain songs played or sung at your service.

Do you want any particular pictures or notices from your past shared at the service (photos, awards, books, things you made, etc.)? Please tell us what you would like placed around for people to view.

Do you want people to do anything special at your service? (Light candles, dance, tell stories, have a picnic, go to a certain spot, have a fund raiser, go on a race together, etc.)

Do you want any swag, gifts, or items given out to people who attend your service? If so, what would you like for them to have? (See GOODBYE) for ideas of items that are commonly given away in honor of the person who died).

Do you want any particular food or drinks served at your service? Please specify what you would like them to consume in honor of you.

Food

Drinks

What other kinds of things would you like, or not like, to happen at your memorial service or funeral?

25

Who You Want To Come To Your Memorial Service

Who do you want to be there or remember you?

There are certain people who are dear to us that we would like to be with us for our final send-off. Some people would want to come and they should be notified that we have passed away. Let them know when and where your celebration of life or funeral will occur.

Immediate family members, including parents, children, and siblings:

Extended family members, including aunts, uncles, cousins, step-families, and other people who are biologically or socially regarded as family

Members of prior families, as in the case of divorce, separation, or other partner relations

Work colleagues, past and present

Professional associations

Civic groups

Military, fraternity, sorority, or other affiliations

Recreational networks

Others you wish to include:

26

People You Don't Want

Who do you NOT want to know that you've died or who you don't want to attend your memorial service?

Let's be honest – unless we are saintly, there are some people that we just don't like and don't want them to know or come. There are people who have been mean or unkind to us. There are those who have done us wrong. There are people that perhaps we have wronged. There may be former lovers or family members who we have intense emotional problems with. We might feel they are two-faced and would come for show or for all the wrong reasons. For whatever reason, there may be some people we don't want to come to say goodbye to us.

Make a list here if there are people you don't want to be notified or who should not be allowed to attend your service.

27

Love Letters

Love Letters you want others to have.

We are loved and we have loved. This is our last opportunity to give people we care about a lasting memento of our care and devotion to them. If there are people you want to write something to, take the time to do this. You can write it here, you can write formal letters or find other ways to say what is in your heart to them. These love letters can be long or short. They could even be just a sentence or two. Or you could draw them a picture or write them a poem. Make it sweet and kind, as they will remember what you say forever. Key people to consider are:

Your parents

Your children

Your siblings

Other relatives

Friends

Spouse

Lovers

And.....????

28

Peace Of Mind Letters

Piece of your mind letters to create Peace of Mind

There may be people in your life that you have been harboring intense feelings about for years that you have never said anything to them about. You have to weigh out whether you want to tell them so or not. In some cases, it may not be a kind thing to do. On the other hand, it may be the right thing for you and for them, for you to get off your chest things that have weighed your heart down. It may be that for countless reasons we haven't felt we could say what we really think to someone, but they need to hear it. Knowing how you feel could help them to reflect and become kinder, better people because of your honesty. Think about the people who keep coming to mind who have upset you for a long time. It's OK for you to have an opportunity to give them a piece of your mind that will give you peace, and curiously may give them an opportunity to make peace as well. After you write out what you wanted to say to them, then you can decide whether you really want to give them to letter or not. Maybe you will. Maybe you will find that just by getting the weight off of your heart that was enough. Again, it's all up to you what you want to do.

29

Letting Go Of Regrets

Your Regrets.

Throughout our lives, most people have some regrets, things that we wish we had done, or things that we are sorry we did. Some people are weighed down by guilt and regret for the rest of their lives. It's time to let them go. Here is a list of regrets that you might have. Instead of blaming and shaming yourself for them, go down the list. If you find that you did any of the following, acknowledge that you did, and then put a mark through it. When you get to the bottom of this long list of possible regrets, you will be instructed on what to do with it.

Handling Anger

I took out my anger on people who are trying to help
I took out my anger on total strangers who happened to be there when I flipped a switch
I blamed others who had nothing to do with the way I felt
I coped by drinking to excess
I coped by taking medication or doing drugs or other substances
I handled weapons
I drove too fast or engaged in road rage
I threw, hit, or broke things

I was physically abusive to others
I said mean things that I shouldn't have said
I was emotionally abusive to others
I set people up to fail
I yelled at a clerk, phone representative, or innocent other
I screamed the TV because I didn't like what I saw or what others were watching
I got annoyed over little things
I rejected and alienated people who care about me and then said things like "see, you never really cared anyway"
I get depressed when things don't go my way
Sometimes I have felt suicidal or tried to hurt myself
I have engaged in self-sabotage
I have been a jerk or asshole

Romantic Relationships

I regret that I picked the wrong partner
Or I stayed too long with them
I'm sorry I let that special someone go
I regret that a special someone let me go
I cared too much and put too much pressure on them
I didn't cherish them enough
I didn't give them a good enough chance
Sorry I didn't say sorry – or wasn't really sorry for things I did
I regret not telling them what I needed or wanted, because if I did maybe things would have been better
I didn't consider their background enough, especially when it came to physical and mental health factors
I came up with excuses for their being lazy, not helpful, not thoughtful, for their substance use, for breaking the law, playing around on us, etc. etc. etc.
I put up with domestic violence

I kept thinking that things would get better, but they didn't

I regret that I didn't stand up for myself and what I believed or wanted

I let myself get lost and I'm sorry

I gave everything and they didn't care and I feel resentful about it

I regret acting like I had family favorites instead of cherishing each person for who they are

Friendships and Peers

I regret being in a certain group or clique

I wish I had stood up to the person who bullied me

I wish I'd listened to my parents and others about not hanging out with certain people

I regret not keeping in touch with certain people who were important to me

I wish I had played more

I regret that I was too judgmental about a person

I wish I had listened more and talked less

I wish their opinion of me didn't matter so much

I regret not helping them when they asked or needed me

I wish I had been more fun

I regret gossiping about them

I am sorry that I didn't have honest conversation with them about the way I felt about things

I wish I had pleased myself instead of always trying to please other people

I am sorry I bought those stupid clothes (got a tattoo, haircut, etc.) in order to make people think I was cool

I regret not treating myself as kindly as I try to treat other people (aka – not taking my own advice)

I regret that I did things to make them like me instead of liking myself more

I regret that I didn't go and see my friend/family member before they died

Physical and Mental Health

I wish I hadn't spent so much time worrying
I wish I had gone to counseling
I am sorry I didn't exercise more
I regret that I let appearance dictate my health decisions
I wish I had more confidence
I regret that I didn't feel as pretty or smart as other people instead of honoring my own unique wonderfulness
I should have taken the medicine or gotten the surgery that the doctor recommended
I should have eaten better
I regret not having gone to the doctor
I am sorry I relied on false information about health
I regret that I didn't know about how trauma can hurt us long-term
I wish I had done my physical therapy exercises more regularly
I wish I hadn't worn those uncomfortable but very fashionable shoes

Education

I wish I had put forth more of an effort to learn in school
I regret thinking that if I was a star athlete that I would get a scholarship and my grades weren't that important
I wish I had taken courses in certain topics
I regret not going to the school I wanted because other people or money pressured me to make a choice that didn't ultimately serve me well

I regret not living in the dorm and missing the normal college experience

I should have finished my degree when I had a chance

I regret cheating in school and not doing my own work

I regret having school loans

I regret not having traveled more and learned about other places

Money

I regret that I never learned money management at home or in school

I didn't pay close attention to what I was spending money on and I'm paying the price for it now

I wish I'd saved more

I regret that I got into debt

I regret buying (or not buying) a house (car, boat, etc.)

I am aware that I made some bad financial choices

I gave away money to people who never paid it back

I regret that I let money run my life decisions and relationships

I wish I hadn't spent so much money on bogus things that were hyped to make me feel better about myself

I regret getting scammed

Career

I regret that I spent too much time at work and not enough at home

I let work be our priority instead of my personal relationships

I'm sorry that even when I was home I was emotionally and physically unavailable because I was obsessed with work stuff

I regret that I stayed at jobs I didn't like just to earn money

I had supervisors who demeaned and ridiculed me because they had the power to do so instead of having the courage to get a different job

I regret that I picked jobs or schools that I thought my parents or partner wanted me to have instead of doing what I really wanted

Parenting

I regret that I didn't listen closely enough to what my children were trying to tell me

I am sorry that I didn't attend certain events that were meaningful to the children because "I was too busy"

I regret that I yelled and didn't show my children how to deal with conflict in a positive way

I am sorry that I taught my children that violence was acceptable

I wish I had realized how fast childhood goes, and once it's gone you can never get it back

I regret not laughing more and teaching them to find the silliness and joy in everyday life

I am sorry that I didn't confront people who said or did mean things to them

My partner was inattentive or abusive to the children and I didn't step in and stop it fast enough, and I am so sorry

I regret not playing outside and doing more things with my children

I am sorry that I kept children busy on screens, TV, and phones instead of teaching them how to play and interact on their own

Other Regrets - Add some that are uniquely yours here.

OK – NOW THAT YOU HAVE GONE THROUGH THE LIST, DO YOU HAVE A LOT OF REGRETS THAT YOU HAVE DRAWN A LINE THROUGH? DID YOU DRAW A LINE THROUGH MOST OR ALL OF THEM? IF YOU DID, THAT'S NORMAL. YOU HAVE CROSSED THEM OFF THE LIST. YOU ACKNOWLEDGED THAT YOU DID OR FELT THESE THINGS.

<u>NOW CROSS THEM OFF IN YOUR MIND.</u>

LET THEM GO!

THEY ARE OVER. THE PAST IS PAST.

YOU COULD SEE YOURSELF AS A HUMAN BEING WHO MAKES MISTAKES – AND YOU LEARN FROM THEM. THAT IS A WONDERFUL TRANSFORMATION. YOU COULD ACKNOWLEDGE THAT EVERYBODY MAKES THESE SAME KINDS OF MISTAKES. IT IS PART OF THE HUMAN CONDITION. IF YOU CONTINUE TO FEEL REGRET AND GUILT, THEN PERHAPS YOU WANT TO REACH OUT AND ENGAGE IN SOME RESTORATIVE JUSTICE AND HEALING. WRITING AN AMENDS LETTER TO THEM COULD BE IN ORDER. SOMETIMES LETTING OTHERS KNOW THAT WE ARE SORRY HELPS THEM TO HEAL. IMPORTANT. SAYING "SORRY" AND REALLY MEANING IT MAY HELP US HEAL TOO.

WHEN YOU SEE ALL THE MARKED-THROUGH ITEMS, IT IS TIME TO FORGIVE YOURSELF. WE SCREWED UP. WE COULD HAVE DONE BETTER. DON'T CARRY THAT WEIGHT AND SADNESS TO YOUR GRAVE. INSTEAD, FOCUS ON THAT WHICH YOU HAVE DONE WELL IN ACTS OF LOVING KINDNESS...

30

Your Good Deeds

Your successes and good deeds are important to remember.

We have done more wonderful, kind, compassionate, good deeds than we can ever count or remember. As we contemplate how we want to say our GoodBye, it is important to think about them. Here are some categories of goodness that you can reflect upon:

Your greatest successes in school (primary, secondary, and beyond)

Your greatest work successes

Successes you have had using your body (health, exercise, sport, weight, etc.)

Successes with relationships (friends, sweethearts, family members, pets, etc.)

Things you're most proud of that few people know about

Something you did that you thought you'd never be able to do

Success in overcoming your own demons

Like the Regret list, now go down this list of possible Successes. Circle the ones that you did or pertain to you. Then, when you get to the bottom of the list, let's chat about what you discovered. Think About:

The fact that you have lived to this day
Times you made someone laugh
Times you played hooky to go have fun
Applied for a job and got it
Saved some money
Bought a car or a house
Was kind to an animal
Sacrificed yourself for someone else's well-being
Gave somebody something that you really would have liked for yourself
Made someone a special meal or food
Had a party for someone
Shutting off lights to save electricity
Learning how to do CPR
Going to a protest for a good cause
Pick up other people's trash that they left on a path
Stood up for someone who was being mistreated
Holding the door for someone
Bought others holiday or birthday gifts
Checked on someone who was sick
Making sure to take poop bags when you walk your dog
Traveled a long distance to help someone
Recycle
Carrying someone's suitcase for them
Answer your phone or greet someone you don't know in a cheerful manner
Volunteered at an organization
Curb your temper
Ask people to talk about themselves and their day without it being about you
Letting someone in a hurry take your place in line
Paying ahead at the toll booth for the person in back of you

Let another driver to merge into your lane instead of getting annoyed
Writing a thank you note
Helped someone move
Went on a march for a cause
Controlled your temper
Did without so someone could have something
Got an award
Earned a good grade
Forgave someone who hurt you
Trusted someone
Graduated
Donated money
Took a chance
Went to counseling
Comforted a friend
Held your tongue
Learned to be more patient
And….

NOW THAT YOU HAVE GONE THROUGH THIS LIST OF SUCCESSES AND GOOD DEEDS, YOU HAVE PROBABLY EXPERIENCED ALL OF THEM. YOU HAVE LIKELY REMEMBERED MANY MORE THAT YOU HAVE SHARED. THE LIST OF THE WAYS THAT INDIVIDUAL LIVES AND THE WORLD AS A WHOLE HAS BENEFITED BECAUSE YOU WERE HERE COULD GO ON TO INFINITY.

YOU MATTER. DO YOU GET IT?

Let go of all the things you didn't do right. Celebrate how the world is a better place, just because you lived and loved.

31

Your Money and Wealth

Your money and wealth

Perhaps one of the most contentious issues to confront as we approach our death is what we are going to do with our financial assets. Who do we want to give them to? Are we giving our inheritance and hard-earned money to our family, to friends, to charitable causes, or to other places? As pointed out in the book, GOODBYE, who gets what can pose tremendous stress and conflict for us, and for those who we leave behind. Most of this information should be included in a legal document, such as a will. That said, you have a lot of thinking to do about who is going to get what, or how much of what you have. Clarification of your assets is important for people to know. Therefore, here are some workbook questions for you to answer that will help others to do what you request.

Do you have your checking accounts?   Yes   No
What banks?

Account numbers

Do you have savings accounts?   Yes   No
What banks?

Account numbers:

Do you have other bank accounts?   Yes   No
Bank
Account

Do you have a retirement account?   Yes   No

Where can it be found?
    Bank or company
    Address
    Account number

Do you have stocks or bonds?   Yes   No

Where can this information be found?

What organization holds it?

What are the account numbers?

Do you have a bank lock box or other safety box where you have put money or valuable assets?   Yes   No
Where is it?
What is the account number

Do you have a key or number to access it - if so, where/what is it?

Do you have any trusts?   Yes   No

What are the names of the trusts and where can they be found?

Who is the trustee of the trust?

Do you own any businesses?   Yes   No

What are their names?

Where are they licensed?

Explain the nature of the business.

Who will be in charge of the business when you pass away?

Name

Contact information.

The business bank holdings – assets, accounts, and debts.

Please put all information of what bank, account numbers, debtors, and other salient information here. Have you stashed or put money (or valuables) in a location that people may not expect? Some people bury it, hide it, put it in odd locations, and it could go undiscovered – or discovered by people you never wanted ot expected to find it. Write down if you have secret spots where you put your money.

Use more pages to clarify your financial holdings so that the people who are left behind know what assets you have, where they are, and how they should access them so they can wrap up your legal affairs.

32

Your Debts

Your debts and what you owe

Most of us owe money to someone when we die. It could be for our house, our car, credit cards, loans, or other bills. In order to take care of your legal affairs, people need to know what you owe to who so they can be paid.

    Do you have a mortgage?   Yes   No

    If yes, what is the mortgage company?
        What is the address/phone of it?
        What is the account number?

    Do you have the deed to your home   Yes   No
        If so, where could it be found?

If you have more than one mortgage, please list the information for all of them.
        Company
        Contact information
        Account information

Do you have a car loan?   Yes   No
    If yes, who is the loan company?
    What is their contact details?
    What is the account number?
If you have paid off your car, where is the title?

Do you own a:
Boat   Yes   No
RV   Yes   No
Motorcycle   Yes   No
Other vehicle?   Yes   No

If you have a loan for any of them, please identify who the lender(s) are, contact information, and account number.

If they are paid off, where is the title to them?

Do you have a student loan?   Yes   No
Who is the lender?
Do you know the account number?
Do you know their phone or address?

List all of your credit cards and their account info:
Credit Card   Account number
1.
2.
3.
4.
5.

What other debts or loans do you have? Please explain what they are, how much, and to whom they should be paid.

Do you owe a person some money? Sometimes we borrow money from individuals. They likely have not forgotten. Make sure to list any people you owe money to so that they can be paid back.

Use the pages here to clarify debs or loan information so that others can make sure your bills are paid.

33

Your Insurance

Insurance details are important for others to take care of you when you're gone.

Most people have several different kinds of insurance policies that will need to be addressed when someone dies. These include life insurance policies, health insurance policies, car insurance policies, and renters or home owners insurance policies. You may have other policies as well. It is important to make sure other people know what the policies are so they can take care of them. Imagine how annoying it could be for people you love to have to chase down all kinds of detailed information like this.

What are your life insurance polices?

Company

Policy number

Company contact phone/address

What is your primary health insurance policy?

Company

Policy number

Company contact

If you have other health insurance policies, please specify below:

Company

Policy number

Company contact

Do you have car insurance? Yes No

If yes, what company has your car insurance?

Policy number

Company contact

Do you have other vehicle insurance? Yes No

(boats, motorcycles, RV, snowmobile, jetski, etc.)

If yes, what is your insurance for?

Company

Policy number

Company contact

Do you have a home owners or rental insurance policy?
Yes   No

If yes, what company has your insurance?

Policy number

Company contact

Other insurance policies and information:

Type of insurance

Company

Policy number

Company contact

Use more pages to explain about other insurance if you want.

34

Your Stuff

Your Stuff

All of us have spent a lifetime accumulating things or "stuff". Some of the things we have taken possession of are really important to us. Other items are just things, useful perhaps but they don't hold any major significance or importance to us. We have many objects that we would actually like to get rid of. There are some items that we have that we might feel really sad if people threw or gave away. What are they? Some items may have more value (monetary or otherwise) than others may know. This is the time to point that out. Here is a list of possible things that people have to decide about. Go down the list and identify if there are special items in the categories that you want to go to someone or someplace in particular.

Furniture:

Cars & Trucks:

Motorcycles, boats, RVs, off-road vehicles, ski-doos, bicycles, etc:

Computer:

TV:

Stereo equipment:

Musical Instruments:

Art:

Books:

Kitchen items, dishes, glassware, etc:

Clothes:

Other items of significance to you:

35

Your Will

Your will

Where there's a will there's a way. A way for you to get what you want. A way for everyone to know what you want them to do. A way to avoid family and business conflicts. If you don't have a will, well, all Hell could break loose. You may not think that you have enough to put in a will. You could assume that everyone would know what you want and that they would negotiate through your death smoothly. You might think that you'll "get around to it" tomorrow. Think again. Whether you are a trillionaire or just scraping by, the reality is that everybody needs a will in order to avoid problems and to take care of the business of wrapping up your life. Wills do not have to be complicated or expensive. You can hire an attorney to make one for you, you can go online and create one, or you can write up what you want and then have it signed by a witness, like a notary public.

Do you already have a will?   Yes   No

If yes, where can your will be found or accessed?

Who do you want to be the executor of your estate, or the person who is charge of carrying out what is in your will, making sure beneficiaries get what they are entitled, paying your bills, and figuring out what to do with your property?

    1st choice: Name of person

    Contact information

    2nd choice: Name of person

    Contact information

    Where is your will going to be so people can find it?

Who are your beneficiaries, and what do you want each of them to have? Perhaps the easiest way may be to use this chart as a guide.

    Person   What to get

Are there charities or organizations that you would like to donate? If so, list them and what you want them to have.

Place to donate   What you want to donate

A will can be designed to contain all kinds of things that you want people to know. Use this section to specify who and what you want. For instance, if you have children, who do you want to be caregivers of them in case you die? If you have pets, where do you want them to live? If you have special items of monetary or sentimental value, who do you want to give them to?

36

Your Obituary

Write your own obituary

When people pass away, it is common to have an obituary or death announcement of the person posted. Typically the funeral home will post one, but obituaries can also be posted in newspapers, put on websites like Facebook, or sent to the organizations, associations, or groups that were a part of the person's life. Sometimes posting these announcements is free, other times they may cost money – and the more you write the more it costs. Think about where you want to obituary to be posted when you write yours.

What should go into an obituary? Here are common things to consider putting into yours:

NAME: Your full name, including your middle name and any name changes or nicknames you may have had.

Birthdate and date when the person died

Loved Ones: This list can be long or short, it all depends on who all you want to include. Typically, a spouse or partner is listed, parents or children, grandchildren, siblings, step-families, former family members, special friends, and pets are listed. Some people list everybody they can think of, others just put broad categories. There's always a concern about forgetting someone, so be thoughtful with creating the list.

Education or Career: Where you went to school, any degrees, jobs, military service, achievements are usually listed. Again, this list could be long or short.

Interests: Hobbies, sports, organizations you've belonged to, religion, favorite things to do – this category gives you the chance to let your personality shine!

Other Things That Are Special About You.

Try writing your obituary here:

37

Your Legacy

What do hope your legacy will be?

As you have gone through this workbook, you have had the opportunity to reflect upon your life. How do you want to be remembered? What is your greatest story that may never have been told? Would you re-write your life if you could? Or are things ending in a way that makes you feel satisfied? Take some time to reflect upon what your journey in this life has been. This is the chance to TELL YOUR STORY THE WAY YOU WANT IT TOLD.

Yvonne Vissing, PhD, is a Clinical Sociologist and Professor of Healthcare Studies at Salem State University in Massachusetts, where she is the founding director of its Center for Childhood & Youth Studies. She is an internationally renowned human rights expert. Dr. Vissing has published over 25 books, including Changing the Paradigm of Homelessness, Women Without Children: Nurturing Lives, Out of Sight, Out of Mind, Children's Human Rights in the USA: Challenges and Opportunities, Re-Imagine Santa, The Santa Spirit Child Welfare in America, and Human Rights Around the Globe. She was a Post-Doctoral Research Fellow at the National Institute of Mental Health and is the founder of a nonprofit organization, The Initiative for Civility in Everyday Life, which houses The World As It Could Be program.

www.ingramcontent.com/pod-product-compliance
Lightning Source LLC
Chambersburg PA
CBHW071958070526
44583CB00015B/1237